STAGING
ASYLUM

Dead Air
for Merlin Luck

Having zipped your lips
shut with the duct
tape you snuck past
the thousand and one lenses,

boos like angry bees
echoed through the studio,
stinging executives.
This was premeditated

murder of television–
you knew and we could tell
by your upwelling, eyes
bloodshot with conviction.

No cheap angel wings
propped up your eviction.
The gobsmacked host
couldn't turn to grist

your expensive silence,
mute shout out to those
like you, we locked up
then voted off the show.

Jaya Savige (from *Surface to Air*, 2011)

STAGING ASYLUM

CONTEMPORARY AUSTRALIAN
PLAYS ABOUT REFUGEES

Edited by **EMMA COX**

First published in 2013
by Currency Press Pty Ltd,
PO Box 2287, Strawberry Hills, NSW, 2012, Australia
enquiries@currency.com.au
www.currency.com.au

CMI (A Certain Maritime Incident) was first published by Currency Press in 2012.

NATIONAL LIBRARY OF AUSTRALIA CIP DATA

Staging asylum : contemporary Australian plays about refugees / edited by Emma Cox.
9780868199832 (paperback)

Notes: Includes bibliographical references.

Contents: Introduction: knowing strangers / Emma Cox—A certain maritime incident / version 1.0—The rainbow dark / Victoria Carless—The Pacific solution / Ben Eltham—Halal-el-mashakel / Linda Jaivin—Journey of asylum – waiting / Catherine Simmonds and members of the Asylum Seeker Resource Centre, Melbourne—Nothing but nothing / Towfiq Al-Qady.

Subjects: Refugees—Drama.

Other Authors/Contributors:
                Cox, Emma, editor.

Dewey Number: A822.4

Contents

Australian Government | Australia Council for the Arts   Publication of this title was assisted by the Commonwealth Government through the Australia Council, its arts funding and advisory body.

Typeset by Claire Grady for Currency Press.
Printed by Openbook Howden, St Marys, SA.
Front cover shows the 2010 Asylum Seeker Resource Centre production of *Journey of Asylum – Waiting* in the Bella Union Theatre, Melbourne (photo: Riza Manalo).
Cover design by Katy Wall for Currency Press.

Introduction: Knowing Strangers

Emma Cox

How do we know a stranger when we see one? How, too, do we know a stranger when she or he is invisible to us? What makes the stranger a person to be wary of, someone from whom we will withhold certain rights, privileges and kindnesses? Cultural theorist Sara Ahmed asks similar questions in her book *Strange Encounters: Embodied Others in Post-Coloniality* (2000), suggesting that strangers are made rather than met, that it is 'relationships of social antagonism that produce the stranger as a figure in the first place' (p. 79). Strangers are also made by relationships of bureaucratic antagonism. In the late capitalist nation, the stranger is a politico-legal category, policed with the aid of passports, visas, body scanners and biometrics. In the case of unauthorised asylum seekers requesting protection from Australia, we can add to that arsenal: the immigration detention centre.

Staging Asylum is the first collection to recognise substantially the role theatre has played in one of Australia's most hotly debated and urgent contemporary issues. If Australia's responses over the last two decades to unauthorised asylum seekers (sometimes tagged pejoratively as 'queue jumpers' or 'illegals') has made anything clear, it is that the emotional force of 'the nation' as an idea manifests in part as sentiments about *what sits outside it*, literally and metaphorically. Political philosopher Giorgio Agamben's work on sovereign power is useful for tracing relationships between collective identification and collective exclusion. Agamben concentrates in particular on the 'camp' of extrajudicial imprisonment. Australia's use of immigration camps for unauthorised asylum seekers began in 1992 with the Paul Keating Labor government's passing of the *Migration Amendment Act*; since that time, the detention of asylum seekers for extended periods has been the most contentious aspect of federal policies of the left and the right. Agamben identifies the paradoxical exclusion and inclusion enacted by the camp, noting that it (p. 40):

is a piece of territory that is placed outside the normal juridical order; for all that however, it is not simply an external space. According to the etymological meaning of the term *exception* (*ex-capere*), what is being excluded in the camp is *captured outside*, that is, it is included by virtue of its very exclusion.

Zones of exclusion are tightly controlled by wealthy nations that, like Australia, have the means to *capture outside*, and thereby to reify their self-fashioning as strong, unified sovereign places.

Each of the six plays in *Staging Asylum* represents a perspective on the politics and debates surrounding unauthorised asylum seekers (mostly 'boatpeople'—those who arrive by means of an aeroplane, not to mention the substantial annual humanitarian intake, don't generate anywhere near as much discussion) in Australia today. The plays were written between 2002 and 2010 and I have sought to encapsulate something of the diversity of theatrical work on asylum, from satire, to knowing and ironic verbatim theatre, to narratives of trauma and self-inflicted violence derived from asylum seekers' stories, to autobiographical as well as community-devised performance.

With the exception of *Journey of Asylum – Waiting* (Trades Hall, Melbourne, 2010), all of the plays in the collection were written and produced during the second half of John Howard's eleven-year leadership of the conservative Liberal–National coalition government (1996–2007). This reflects the fact that a flurry of theatrical work about asylum seekers and refugees was produced in Australia in the four or five years following 2001. It was a period that saw the ratcheting up of Labor's 1992 legislation with controversial, hard-line deterrence policies of maritime return, territorial excision and offshore detention at far-flung facilities on Christmas Island, Nauru and Manus Island in Papua New Guinea. (For more information on the gradual expansion of excision legislation, see my introduction to Ben Eltham's *The Pacific Solution*, p. 69.) But the politicisation of asylum seekers shows no sign of waning. At the time of writing (July 2013), the newly reappointed Prime Minister, Kevin Rudd, has announced a radical plan to resettle all unauthorised asylum seekers in Papua New Guinea, ensuring that Australia's annual humanitarian intake of 20,000 people will be offered only to those registered in UN refugee camps. If part of the impetus for the playwrights featured in *Staging Asylum* was, in their most utopian moments, the hope of contributing to social mobilisation and perhaps ultimately to policy change, then what are we to make of the plays from the vantage point of 2013, when years after the Howard government's demise, Ministers on the opposing side are heralding an era of ever tougher asylum policy?

For me, the answer lies in the idea that political theatre, like other political arts, doesn't function as an intravenous drug to the bloodstream of body politic, an antidote to perceived legislative ills. And in most cases, politically motivated writing isn't produced with the aim of ending up on a politician's desk (though such an image is worth pausing over!). Writers (as well as directors, actors, producers and others) respond to the high-stakes, deeply felt terrain of the political because they must. Because they're members of a society. Part of the playwright's job, and theatre's, is to ask questions, to dramatise certain habits of thought and practice, not to set down answers or plans. Social changes outside the theatre space are going to be incremental rather than seismic, and may take the form of therapeutic ends for former detainees who, like Iraqi writer and painter Towfiq Al-Qady, write or perform their own stories, or of conviviality in day-to-day interactions across cultures. Change may also, indeed, mean that Ministerial and Prime Ministerial discourse that at the start of the twenty-first century expressed repugnance toward 'people like that'—lip-sewing, child-endangering, patience-testing strangers—now tends to concentrate more on regional security and the prevention of tragic deaths at sea. (And so we return again to the governmental.)

While all the plays in this collection are concerned, one way or another, with what cross-cultural engagement looks like, in some cases they are oriented more towards the ongoing cultural conversation Australians are having with one another, than with asylum seekers. This is true of version 1.0's ironic verbatim text, *CMI (A Certain Maritime Incident)* (Performance Space, Sydney, 2004) and Victoria Carless's domestic satire, *The Rainbow Dark* (Metro Arts Theatre, Brisbane, 2006), neither of which features any characters who are asylum seekers or refugees, and to a large extent Ben Eltham's dark satire, *The Pacific Solution* (Metro Arts Theatre, Brisbane, 2006). This is not to say that these plays are insular in their orientation, by any means. Rather, version 1.0, Carless and Eltham recognise that, ultimately, asylum legislation reveals more about Australia and Australians than it does about asylum seekers, and that the fate of asylum seekers is tied umbilically with the question of what it means to be (and behave as) a citizen in a liberal democratic nation that is a signatory to the UN Refugee Convention and Protocol.

In contrast, Linda Jaivin's short play, *Halal-el-Mashakel* (Old Fitzroy Hotel Theatre, Sydney, 2003) and the longer episodic text, *Journey of Asylum – Waiting*, devised by Catherine Simmonds and members of the Asylum Seeker Resource Centre (ASRC) in Melbourne, take on the tricky task of placing asylum seekers and refugees centre stage, of transforming the actual experiences of individuals without reproducing (and reducing) refugee identity to unremitting tragedy and suffering. Both works emerged out of relationships of trust and reciprocity nurtured over time: Jaivin's play was inspired by the bonds she developed with detainees during an intensive period spent visiting Villawood immigration detention centre in western Sydney, while *Journey of Asylum – Waiting* was a collectively devised project performed by Australian and refugee participants. *Halal-el-Mashakel* is underpinned by the author's determination to speak on behalf of those 'locked up in our detention centres', while the ASRC's work seeks to weave wide-ranging stories into a multivocal, sometimes surreal whole.

Al-Qady's *Nothing But Nothing* (Metro Arts Theatre, Brisbane, 2005) is the only play in *Staging Asylum* created solely by a former asylum seeker (now a new Australian citizen). Rarely do asylum seekers and refugees find the opportunity to write, perform and co-direct their own work in a professional context, as Al-Qady did. A piece of intersubjective autobiography that speaks emotionally of his own experience as well as those of his family and fellow Iraqi citizens, Al-Qady's play is one that expresses an indestructible capacity for hope.

Obviously, no single play in this book can encompass Australia's cultural and political landscape concerning asylum seekers and refugees. But side-by-side, they represent a small cluster of voices that remember where we have been and invite us to imagine where we might be heading as a nation that must continue to encounter and respond to strangers.

CMI

(A Certain Maritime Incident)

VERSION 1.0

From left: Danielle Antaki as Senator Bartlett, Stephen Klinder as Senator Cook, Deborah Pollard as Senator Faulkner and Christopher Ryan as Senator Collins in the 2004 production of CMI (A Certain Maritime Incident) *in The Performance Space, Sydney. (Photo: Heidrun Löhr.)*

Introduction

On or around 6 October 2001, a distressed Suspected Illegal Entry Vessel, SIEV 4, carrying 223 asylum seekers, was intercepted and its passengers rescued north of Christmas Island by the Australian Navy vessel HMAS *Adelaide*. The rescue acquired its misnomer, the 'children overboard' affair, after Navy personnel, senior government ministers and the Prime Minister circulated the claim that asylum seekers had thrown children into the water to manipulate Navy rescuers and secure passage to Australia. The claim lit up the media and the record wasn't set straight until well after the Howard government was reappointed with an increased majority in the following month's general election.

It says a lot about 2001 that 'children overboard' doesn't rank decisively top of the list of Australia's asylum seeker-related infamy that year. But it so happened that in August 2001 the Norwegian freighter, MV *Tampa*, helmed by Captain Arne Rinnan, rescued several hundred asylum seekers in international waters and proceeded to defy Australian government orders by entering Australian territorial waters, thereby setting in motion a series of fast-track legislative measures—including offshore detention of asylum seekers on Christmas Island, Nauru and Manus Island and the excision of migration territory—that were to be known as the Pacific Solution. It was also in 2001 when an unknown asylum seeker vessel, 'SIEV X' (X because the vessel was never numbered), sank between Australia and Indonesia, resulting in the deaths of 353 people.

Sydney performance collective version 1.0's *CMI (A Certain Maritime Incident)* touches on the SIEV X tragedy, but it's the 'children overboard' fiasco, which occurred only a fortnight earlier, that is the play's primary subject matter. The verbatim work was first produced at Sydney's Performance Space in 2004 and it toured to The Street Theatre, Canberra, later that year.

The bulk of the text was devised by version 1.0 members out of the screeds of Hansard tabled from the Australian Senate Select Committee on A Certain Maritime Incident. The Committee, which sat in 2002, was comprised of Labor, Liberal, Democrat and Independent senators and dealt primarily with the children overboard incident, though SIEV X also came under its purview. Of the former, the Committee concluded in its executive summary that 'No children were thrown overboard from SIEV 4' (p. xxiii). Of the latter, it reported: 'the Committee finds it extraordinary that a major human disaster could occur in the vicinity of a theatre of intensive Australian operations, and remain undetected until three days after the event, without any concern being raised within intelligence and decision making circles' (p. xlii). Of course, various witnesses and politicians said an awful lot more besides.

Verbatim theatre, which is devised from transcribed testimonies (usually interviews, statements or inquiries), has emerged as one of the most prominent modes of representing refugees' and asylum seekers' stories on stage; indeed it has become, in Britain, the US and Canada, as well as Australia, generic shorthand for truth-telling in political theatre on a range of topics. *CMI* questions, brilliantly, the naturalised link between testimonies and historical events with its manipulation of verbatim material and its problematisation of acts of remembering, recording and speaking.

But it doesn't do this simply in order to be clever. The political bite of *CMI* derives from the way Navy personnel, government ministers and committee senators used language that was prevaricating, posturing, speculative and even at times downright false. As version 1.0 member and one of the play's performers, David Williams, commented, 'The Liberal senators behave shockingly, they stonewall and deny and waste time, but the Labor Party doesn't care about the asylum seekers, it just wants to embarrass the government' (quoted in Justin Norrie's review of *CMI* in *The Sydney Morning Herald* on 26 March 2004, p. 15).

Faced with an historical record that reads in part like self-parody, the play's creators inserted gaps between subjects and performers. This approach sets *CMI* apart from the documentary realist mode of presentation usually favoured in verbatim theatre. One such insertion comes in the first scene, when a small child, accompanied by an interviewer, reads a transcript from a radio interview with then Minister for Defence, Peter Reith:

MR REITH: […] these photos show absolutely without question whatsoever that there were children in the water. Now we have a number of people, obviously RAN people who were there who reported the children were thrown into the water. Now you may want to question the veracity of reports of the Royal Australian Navy. I don't and I didn't either but I have subsequently been told that they have also got film. That film is apparently on HMAS *Adelaide*. I have not seen it myself and apparently the quality of it is not very good, and it's infra-red or something but I am told that someone has looked at it and it is an absolute fact, children were thrown into the water. So do you still question it?

The child's account is evaluated on a lie detector, which delivers a 'truth' reading, or at least, this is implied when the interviewer praises the child-as-Reith for having spoken the words 'much better than you did last time'. The scene not only exemplifies what performance theorist Peggy Phelan has described as our era's 'condition of witnessing what one did not (and perhaps cannot) see' (p. 577), but also suggests that truth-telling is something that can be rehearsed and crafted until it may be said to 'pass'.

Having not been extended legal immunity, asylum seekers did not testify for the Select Committee. version 1.0 approaches the problem of embodying these absent subjects in a sophisticated way. While on the one hand, the Australian characters become more and more crazily surreal, on the other, asylum seekers are distilled at the beginning and end of the play as 'dead', naked bodies prepared for mortuary storage, and in the closing moments as a computerised rendering of translated testimonies from SIEV X survivors. The play's final irony is this: the mechanising of voices only reinforces the plea for human validation that compels these horrific accounts.

Emma Cox

CMI (A Certain Maritime Incident) was first produced by version 1.0 at The Performance Space, Sydney, on 26 May 2004 with the following participants:

Performers:
Danielle Antaki, Nikki Heywood, Stephen Klinder, Deborah Pollard, Christopher Ryan, David Williams, with Frank Dwyer, Ren Khava, Minna McClure (alternating)

Devised by the performers and Paul Dwyer

Producer, David Williams
Dramaturgy, Dr Paul Dwyer

CHARACTERS

HON. PETER REITH, Defence Minister

VIRGINIA TRIOLI, ABC radio presenter

VICE-ADMIRAL DAVID SHACKLETON, Chief of Navy, Royal Australian Navy

SENATOR PETER COOK (ALP, Western Australia), Chair, Senate Select Committee on a Certain Maritime Incident

SENATOR JOHN FAULKNER (ALP, New South Wales)

SENATOR GEORGE BRANDIS (Liberal, Queensland)

SENATOR BRETT MASON (Liberal, Queensland)

SENATOR ANDREW BARTLETT (Australian Democrats, Queensland)

SENATOR JACINTA COLLINS (ALP, Victoria)

COMMANDER NORMAN BANKS, Captain of HMAS *Adelaide*, Royal Australian Navy

REAR ADMIRAL GEOFFREY SMITH, Maritime Commander, Royal Australian Navy

JANE HALTON, Chair, People Smuggling Taskforce, Department of the Prime Minister and Cabinet

TONY KEVIN, former Australian diplomat

DANIELLE ANTAKI, performer, version 1.0

NIKKI HEYWOOD, performer, version 1.0

STEPHEN KLINDER, performer, version 1.0

DEBORAH POLLARD, performer, version 1.0

CHRISTOPHER RYAN, performer, version 1.0

DAVID WILLIAMS, performer, version 1.0

PROLOGUE

The theatre doors open. The audience enters through a single corridor down the centre of the theatre space. Along the corridor are a number of naked bodies prepared for mortuary storage that the audience has to step over to reach their seats. At the end of the corridor is a small child with a minder. Behind them is an enormous Australian flag, hung upside down. After the audience has navigated the bodies, and taken their seats, an interview begins. MR REITH *is played by the child, and tested on a lie detector by the* INTERVIEWER.

INTERVIEWER [Stephen]: Come on, Mr Reith. Mr Reith, this is the lie detector. I'll just turn that on for you. Do you want to just talk into the microphone and say, 'Hello, I'm Mr Reith'?

REITH [child]: Hello, I'm Mr Reith.

INTERVIEWER: Very good. Now, Mr Reith, you have something to say, don't you?

REITH: Yes. Well, it did happen. The fact is the children were thrown into the water. We got that report within hours of that happening. Given that there are people who weren't there of course, you know, claiming all sorts of, making all sorts of exaggerated claims.

INTERVIEWER: Mr Reith, there's nothing in this photo that indicates these people either jumped or were thrown.

REITH: No, well you are now questioning the veracity of what has been said. Those photos are produced as evidence of the fact that there were people in the water. You're questioning whether it even happened, that's the first point and I just want to answer that by saying that these photos show absolutely without question whatsoever that there were children in the water. Now we have a number of people, obviously RAN people, who were there who reported the children were thrown into the water. Now you may want to question the veracity of reports of the Royal Australian Navy. I don't and I didn't either, but I have subsequently been told that they have also got film. That film is apparently on HMAS *Adelaide*. I have not seen it myself and apparently the quality of it is not very good, and it's infra-red or something, but I am told that someone has looked at it

and it is an absolute fact, children were thrown into the water. So do
you still question it?

INTERVIEWER: Thank you, Minister Reith. That was much better than
you did last time. See you later, Mr Reith.

The CHILD *exits.*

Unfortunately, Mr Reith wasn't able to stay with us for the inquiry, as
he had to catch a flight to London.

ACT 1: FOGS OF WAR

*Music begins. A timeline of events leading up to the 'children overboard'
incident scrolls on an overhead projector:*

> *13 JUNE 2001: RUDDOCK IN JAKARTA TO MEET EMBASSY
> STAFF AND DISCUSS DISRUPTION OF PEOPLE SMUGGLING,
> ETC.*

> *26 AUGUST 2001: MV* TAMPA *RESCUES ASYLUM SEEKERS
> FROM THE PALAPA AT THE REQUEST OF AUSTRALIAN RESCUE
> AUTHORITIES.*

> *27 AUGUST 2001: CABINET DECIDES NOT TO ALLOW* TAMPA
> *TO DISEMBARK PASSENGERS AT CHRISTMAS ISLAND; JANE
> HALTON CONVENES PEOPLE SMUGGLING TASKFORCE.*

> *28 AUGUST 2001: JOHN HOWARD ON 'A CURRENT AFFAIR':
> 'WE ARE A HUMANE PEOPLE. OTHERS KNOW THAT AND
> THEY SOMETIMES TRY TO INTIMIDATE US WITH OUR OWN
> DECENCY.' OPERATION RELEX ESTABLISHED.*

> *11 SEPTEMBER 2001.*

> *4 OCTOBER 2001: TROOPS COMMITTED TO 'WAR ON TERROR'
> IN AFGHANISTAN; SHIPS SENT TO GULF.*

> *5 OCTOBER 2001: ELECTION CALLED FOR 10 OCTOBER.*

> *6 OCTOBER 2001: HMAS* ADELAIDE *STARTS SHADOWING
> SIEV 4.*

> *7 OCTOBER 2001: 01:39 GMT, WARNINGS TO HEAVE TO;
> BETWEEN 03:59 GMT AND 04:20 GMT, WARNING SHOTS; 04:30
> GMT, BOARDING PARTY TURNS BOAT BACK TO INDONESIA.*

7 OCTOBER 2001: ABOUT 5:00 A.M., MAN OVERBOARD, CHILD HELD UP NEAR RAILING. 14 PEOPLE JUMP OVERBOARD BETWEEN 05:00 A.M. AND 06:00 A.M.

7 OCTOBER 2001: SILVERSTONE CALLS BANKS IN THE MIDST OF OPERATION (EXACT TIME DISPUTED). SILVERSTONE'S (AMENDED) NOTES SUGGEST BANKS SAID SOMETHING ABOUT A KID OR KIDS OVERBOARD; BANKS IS ADAMANT HE DIDN'T.

7 OCTOBER 2001: APPROX. 7:30 A.M. SILVERSTONE CALLS TITHERIDGE AND REAR ADMIRAL SMITH. TITHERIDGE CALLS HALTON SEVERAL TIMES 08:00 A.M., AND 09:00 A.M. HALTON SHARES REPORT OF CHILDREN OVERBOARD WITH PST; RUDDOCK CALLS PST TO SPEAK TO BILL FARMER (SECRETARY OF DIMIA) AND GETS THE REPORT. RUDDOCK MAKES IT PUBLIC.

8 OCTOBER 2001: THE STORY IS ON THE FRONT PAGE OF PAPERS; SIEV 4 SINKS.

10 OCTOBER 2001: RUDDOCK PUBLISHES PHOTOS.

19 OCTOBER 2001: SIEV X SINKS. 353 PEOPLE DROWN.

AND SO ON...!

The upside down flag falls to reveal a large table and a group of SENATORS. *The* SENATORS *seat themselves and the table moves slowly downstage. As the table arrives* ADMIRAL SHACKLETON, *Chief of the Royal Australian Navy, steps up to the microphone.*

SHACKLETON [Danielle]: On eight November 2001 I attended the departure of HMAS ships *Kanimbla* and *Adelaide* for operations in the Persian Gulf area. I visited *Adelaide* and spent about 30 minutes with Commander Banks, the commanding officer. He described the circumstances of six, seven and eight October, and I watched the videotape taken by the ship using its camera system. There was no evidence I could see on that tape of people being thrown into the water, but there was a person holding a child over the side with what I viewed as being the clear intent to do so. It is easy to see that in the heat of the action there could have been an assessment of people being thrown into the water. This is why it takes time to get clarity and understanding of fast-moving events. Subsequent analysis of the activities undertaken by the crew of the *Adelaide* change the original assessment by Banks. This is not unusual. Commander Banks told me on eight November that he then advised CJTF 639—that's the Commander of the Joint Task Force 639—via radio telephone on about nine October, of the changed assessment of these events—that is, that children were not thrown in the water. This brings me back to the evidence I gave to the Senate on the 20th of February 2002, when I was asked about the 'fog of war'. My answer was:

> DANIELLE *pulls out a brightly coloured beer coaster from her pocket, and reads from it. Her voice deepens and slows. The music volume increases.*

It is related to the reality that everything is real but it is not real. You are trying to pull threads and strands from many miscellaneous and sometimes disconnected information flows. You are trying to build a puzzle from many disconnected pieces. Sometimes the pieces fit accurately, sometimes they do not. You are dealing with millions of shades of grey and it is only as events start to get to a point of culmination that they start to form up into a real pattern, and then sometimes it disintegrates again as the events change. This is constantly moving and going up and down all the time. The commanding officer has to make hypotheses, judgments and calls based on what he sees at the time. It is never absolutely right; it is never absolutely wrong.

The music cuts abruptly.

This is what I call 'the fog of war'.

BRANDIS [Nikki]: Most eloquent, Admiral.

SHACKLETON: Thank you.

CHAIR [Stephen]: Why didn't you contradict the minister?

SHACKLETON: Because Defence had told the minister that children had been thrown into the water, and I was not contradicting that advice.

CHAIR: But you knew—Senator Faulkner took you through this earlier today—that people had not been thrown into the water. If you are sitting there and you know that what the minister is saying is not true, why do you have to then fall into line and not contradict him?

SHACKLETON: It was not a case of what the minister thought was true or not; it was a case of what the minister had been told. I did not know what the minister had been told, other than that children had been thrown into the water.

CHAIR: We are misunderstanding each other, Vice-Admiral Shackleton. You knew that they had not been thrown into the water; why didn't you simply say they had not been?

SHACKLETON: My opinion at that stage of the game was that they probably had not been thrown into the water. I had not talked to the CDF—that's the Chief of the Defence Force—since I had returned to the country, so I did not know what the minister had been told in the interim. It was not my place to make public statements about these sorts of issues in this particular instance unless the minister gave me approval to do so.

CHAIR: I know it has been a long day, and let us pray it will shortly close, but this is where I have some problem, Vice-Admiral, to be honest with you. You knew that the report was that no children had been thrown in the water, that the photographs that had been exhibited in the media which purported to be evidence were not true—they were of another event—and that the video was inconclusive. So you had in your possession pretty decisive information about what had happened and, while I can understand that you did not know what the minister knew, it seems to me that you were much closer to the source and did know. Is it because of this order that authorises people who can and cannot speak about these things you felt you were outside of those orders?

SHACKLETON: At that stage of the game, yes.

CHAIR: Excuse me, one moment, Admiral Shackleton.

> CHRIS RYAN *walks over to an overhead projector and displays the following text:*
> *WE KNOW THAT YOU KNOW WE ARE NOT REALLY THE SENATORS WHO TOOK PART IN THE CMI SENATE INQUIRY. STEPHEN IS A LOT SHORTER THAN SENATOR COOK AND DEBORAH WHO PLAYS SENATOR FAULKNER IS ACTUALLY A WOMAN. WE FOUND THAT OUT AFTER THE AUDITION.*

FAULKNER [Deborah]: Vice-Admiral, I would like to ask you about the 'fog of war', because I, too, am interested in this. I agree with Senator Brandis that what you said about the 'fog of war' was indeed most eloquent. Does the 'fog of war' lead one to a conclusion or suggestion that an initial report that you might receive from a commander—in this case Commander Banks—might often be incorrect or require further examination? Is that something that the 'fog of war' would lead you to be cautious about initial reports?

SHACKLETON: Yes. Certainly if you know that the circumstances are very demanding and that the reports are what I would call 'snapshots in time', there is a reasonable probability that they will not be factually accurate.

FAULKNER: So what kind of burden of proof do you think applies to corrections to commanders' initial reports?

SHACKLETON: They have the same burden of proof as to the formation of the original report in the first instance.

FAULKNER: Now, I am interested in your view on this, because you raised with senators the issue of the 'fog of war'. I am reminded about the CDF's evidence—in which I think he described it as 'a principle of war'—that the commander's initial report could only be contradicted by compelling evidence. There seems to be a bit of a difference here.

SHACKLETON: We place great faith in our commanding officers to make calls as they see it and for those calls—by which I mean, reports—to be informed by all of their experience in interpreting the circumstances as they see around them. But, even then, it is true to say that often the first call is the right call, even though doubts start to come into your mind later on.

BRANDIS: Admiral Shackleton, could I take up that very point, if I may? We speak about the first call being the right call, but the use of the word 'call' implies a judgment.

SHACKLETON: Yes.

BRANDIS: But here we are not talking about a judgment, are we? What we are talking about is a description of what somebody saw. What is relevant is: did the man see what he says he saw or didn't he? Context, which might affect judgment, does not affect mere description. Would you accept that proposition?

SHACKLETON: I think in these circumstances, where he would have been watching a boat with people moving around—and he may have seen something out of the corner of his eye or he may have seen something which he then said 'that represents somebody being thrown over the side'—I think that is both an observation and an assessment of what it meant.

BRANDIS: Accepting what you say, as I do, nevertheless, whether it be an observation or an assessment, it is merely the description of an observed phenomenon—something somebody saw. And even though what he saw he may have seen imperfectly, the proposition I am putting to you is that he will never be in a better position to make that assessment or to say what he saw than he is at the moment he is seeing it.

SHACKLETON: Agreed.

BRANDIS: That is the distinction between narration and recollection. Narration does not depend upon memory and it does not depend upon reconstruction or it does not depend upon doubts, or a man working something over and over in his mind, whereas recollection does. Would you agree?

SHACKLETON: I would agree with that.

BRANDIS: Thank you, Vice-Admiral Shackleton.

> SHACKLETON *leaves the microphone.*

FAULKNER: Anyway, what I was trying to do…

CHAIR: I do not want to cut you off, Senator Faulkner, but we are getting into a situation where this is ping-ponging backwards and forwards, and I now want to clamp down a bit and give a bit of form to it. I think we are getting down to ontological truth—whether you actually saw it or were you really dreaming!

BARTLETT [Danielle]: Whether we all exist.

CHAIR: Thank you, Senator Bartlett. Commander Banks is waiting to come on. He is the person who was there; maybe these questions are best left to him. I am not saying they cannot be asked but, in weighing the value of them, maybe they are best left to him. We should ask Banks. When he is done with his pizza, after dinner, we will. Proceedings suspended from 6:51 p.m. to 8:17 p.m.

> *There is a short suspension. The acting* SENATORS *slump on the table, and the* CHAIR *holds a large clock with which he manually*

moves the hands forward from 6:51 p.m. to 8:17 p.m. He puts the clock down and proceedings resume.

Enter COMMANDER NORMAN BANKS, *Royal Australian Navy.*

I will ask Senator Bartlett to commence the batting. Before I do that, though, I have just one question: were any children thrown overboard?

BANKS [David]: I was going to make a statement, if I could, and I will answer that question.

CHAIR: Please proceed to make that statement.

BANKS: Distinguished senators, I am Commander Norman Stewart Banks. I make this statement in my capacity as the commanding officer of HMAS *Adelaide*. As a career professional, I would ask the honourable senators to respect that I am unashamedly apolitical and that I cannot and will not make comment on matters of government policy. I will, however, speak freely about the events of six to ten October 2001 and the circumstances surrounding what became known as SIEV 4—that's Suspected Illegal Entry Vessel 4—or, as you know it, 'a certain maritime incident'. The events of SIEV 4 were by their very nature extremely significant and, even without the subsequent furore and the repeated investigations, the rescue of 223 unauthorised arrivals by HMAS *Adelaide* would always have stayed in my immediate recall as a most memorable incident. It would not be a Senate appearance by me without photographs. These are a 'best of' selection, which in my mind will set the scene and add some context to your deliberations. With your leave, Mr Chair, I will present the photographs.

CHAIR: As there is no objection, leave is granted.

BANKS: They are numbered one to thirty-one, and I will draw attention to them as we go through. On Saturday, six October, at about 1350 Golf—that's the time zone that takes place around Christmas Island—HMAS *Adelaide*, in response to shore-based secret intelligence cueing, intercepted a critical contact of interest 100 nautical miles north of Christmas Island. The 20- to 25-metre wooden-hulled vessel initially flew an Indonesian national flag. Of note, the personnel on board were all wearing life jackets. One of the photos is numbered one and it shows a number of, in your vernacular, SUNCs—Suspected Unauthorised Non-Citizens—I think the term now is UAs 'Unauthorised Arrivals'. You can see it's darkness and you can see they are wearing life jackets. In this photo you can see no signs of distress.

FAULKNER: Where did you say that photo was taken from?

BANKS: It was taken from the long-range RHIB, that's a rigid-hulled inflatable boat, a 7.2-metre boat, and it has a crew of two. At 0139G Golf, on Sunday, seven October, the SIEV altered course towards Christmas Island, the lights of which were now becoming visible on the horizon. By 0230 Golf, the SIEV entered the Australian contiguous zone. From 0300G Golf, warnings to heave-to were passed in English and Bahasa by radio and loudhailer both from *Adelaide* and the alongside RHIB, and communications were also attempted in Lebanese and Arabic by a sailor of Lebanese origin. I commenced action to compel the SIEV to heave-to to allow my boarding party to embark and eventually commenced firing aimed warning shots ahead of the vessel at 0359 Golf and again at 0409 Golf, 0416 Golf and 0420 Golf.

He fires warning shots over the head of the SENATORS *with a small cap gun. They slump in their chairs, playing dead.*

CHAIR: Senators, the TV news deadline has passed. You can turn away from your theatrics. Carry on, Commander.

The 'dead' SENATORS *sit upright again.*

BANKS: The boarding party of nine estimated there were 250 unauthorised arrivals on board. The boarding party reported that they were angry, disappointed, making veiled threats to commit suicide, gesturing with wooden sticks and being very vocal. One unauthorised arrival jumped overboard but was promptly recovered by the RHIB.

STEPHEN: [*to the sound operator*] Matt, Dave, this is going on too long. Can we fast forward a bit to CMI page 143?

DAVID flicks forward several pages in BANKS' *statement, then continues delivering the statement.*

BANKS: At 0539 Golf, sunrise took place. This was the period of morning twilight, so darkness had become dawn and was becoming sunrise, but the ambient light was such that it was all clearly visible by the naked eye. Photo number two shows some of the SUNCs on top of the coach-house preparing to jump overboard. Photos three and four are general photos of *Adelaide*. There I am trying to provide more presence and assert my control. You can see that there are a number of people on the coach-house—some of whom subsequently jumped—and the beginnings of the stages of a man dressing a child in a life jacket at the end of the coach-house.

COLLINS [Chris]: Commander, is the child still at the top?

BANKS: Not in photo eight. In photo six the child is still sitting on the coach-house. In photo seven the child has been returned inside the coach-house and those are some of the unauthorised arrivals who came up and helped move that father—the man I assume to be her father—and child back inside.

STEPHEN: Matt, Dave. Again. Can we fast forward a bit again, to CMI page 164?

> DAVID *flicks forward several more pages in* BANKS' *statement, then continues delivering the statement at a slightly faster pace.*

BANKS: I guess some of my photos are out of sequence now. Fourteen unauthorised arrivals jumped or were thrown overboard. I use the words 'thrown overboard' here advisedly. Those were the words used in my signal and reported repeatedly. The SIEV and the SUNCs were directed to Indonesia… which is… that way. [*He points roughly north-west.*] They were shown a chart, and I also provided a hand-held compass to assist them with that. They had earlier thrown their own compass overboard.

> *The conference table begins to spin, and the* SENATORS *attempt to maintain their position at the table.* BANKS *follows the table as it spins, increasing his pace as the table spinning gets faster.*

We towed the vessel for the next 22 hours without incident. The next photographs, 14 to 23, go through the subsequent sinking of the SIEV on eight October, the day after the man overboard incident. The embarked Navy steaming party of 11 effected what I called a 'controlled abandon ship' from SIEV 4. *Adelaide* launched six 25-man life rafts and, commenced a rescue of the unauthorised arrivals, all of whom were now in the water.

BARTLETT: It seems to me that once a vessel is in that condition, why wait for it to sink? Wouldn't it have been easier—I acknowledge the magnificent efforts of people in rescuing everybody without loss of life—to get them all off before the thing sank rather than wait for it to sink, as it almost inevitably seemed likely to do? It does not sound from those descriptions that it would have been safe to wave it off back to Indonesia.

BANKS: Photograph 14 shows that the vessel went bow down very rapidly. You can see the sea-state a little clearer in this shot—and there is a slight sea-state. Some of the luggage started to float out of the SIEV and the people—in a natural panic—began to move around the SIEV and affect the vessel's stability. Photo 15 shows the SIEV is now nose down and the forward RHIB has just extracted an infant from the port side of the SIEV. People on board the SIEV were concerned. They passed the baby to our RHIB and we took it away as one of the first people off the SIEV. Photo 17 shows the situation deteriorating.

The table spins increasingly faster. There is much chaos. BANKS *is forced to run after the table to continue his testimony.* DEBORAH *signals 'baby overboard' to the audience in semaphore with a flag and a toy baby.*

We put a ladder in the water, we put a cargo net in the water, we put a Billy Pugh rescue strop in the water, and we had a Nowra strop in the water. Whilst we could not understand their plight, we had to treat them as refugees. I was particularly proud of that shift in attitude of the ship's company when this situation developed into a humanitarian assistance task; the performance of the ship's company of *Adelaide* to make this rescue happen was unparalleled and can best be described by the simple superlative 'superb'. In response to questions about media misrepresentation, I gathered testimony from the ship's company of HMAS *Adelaide*. These statements were made by people who had witnessed the man overboards on seven October. This was done to put to rest false media claims that children had been thrown overboard.

BANKS *runs downstage to the microphone.*

In summary, by 10 October, it was clear to the Commanding Officer *Adelaide*, Commander Joint Task Force 639, and the Maritime Commander Australia that no children had been thrown overboard, and that no signal originating from HMAS *Adelaide* had ever

referred to an incident involving children being thrown overboard.
Thank you, Senators.

> *The table stops spinning. An overhead projection slide is displayed:*
> *NO TABLES WERE SPUN DURING THE CMI INQUIRY. EXCEPT*
> *PERHAPS THE TEA TROLLEY. BUT THIS IS SPECULATION, NOT*
> *FACT.*

BRANDIS: Commander, can I suggest to you with respect—that, being
aware of this incident, you were being very careful not to be
remembering or be seen to be claiming more than you could in fact
remember, which is why you, as I said before, quite properly qualified
yourself by the use of words like 'possibly'. It is dishonest to say
'I remember something' when I am not sure about it; it is very honest
to say 'I am not sure about it, but possibly it happened'. I take it that
this statement of yours is in the second of those two categories—a
qualified concession of the imperfections of memory.

BANKS: I did a data dump.

> *The* SENATORS *all laugh.*

I did a data dump and then sat down to proofread and structure this
with those qualifications, to try to make absolutely sure that there
was nothing in here that could be misconstrued or lead people down
the garden path.

COLLINS: Is there any record of reports of children in the water?

BRANDIS: Excuse me, Senator Collins.

COLLINS: He is saying that he did a data dump.

BRANDIS: Senator Collins!

COLLINS: I am trying to understand what he means.

BRANDIS: I have been so patient with the Labor senators, but I have only
got 25 minutes and I would like to get to the end—

COLLINS: You will have more time.

BRANDIS: —of my cross-examination of the witness by four o'clock.

CHAIR: You are not cross-examining them, Senator Brandis.

BRANDIS: Well, my examination of—

CHAIR: This is not a court.

BANKS: If I could help Senators, the term 'data dump' means that I put
all my thoughts and words onto the laptop; it means that I dump my
memory.

SENATOR BRANDIS *pulls out a gun and points it at* BANKS.

BRANDIS: But what if it were a grey area? Perhaps it was a little unfair to you, Commander Banks, in the 'fog of war'. It is unfair to you, isn't it, that a black-and-white answer should be demanded of you in relation to a confused and highly mobile series of events of which you witnessed only some?

BANKS: I think four days later it was clear that a black-and-white answer was warranted and was achievable.

SENATOR COOK *pulls out a gun and points it at* BRANDIS.

CHAIR: This question about the fog of war has it that people can get confused in the heat of the moment—which I think is what this fog of war idea seems to be about. Your training over 25 years is about being as clear and as precise as possible in difficult circumstances, among other things, isn't it?

BANKS: Yes, it is. The fog of war issue has been on my mind a little bit. The fog of war relates more to a threat to the ship or to people. There was no threat to HMAS *Adelaide* or our people during that event. We were in control of the situation. So I do not think the fog of war applied, and it is other people's expression, not mine.

CHAIR: Here we are conducting a war—and Australia is part of this—against countries which have tyrannical regimes which are not democratic, which suppress their people's liberties and rights and which engage in or are associated with international terrorism. The people on SIEV 4 were fleeing from those regimes, were they not?

BANKS: Yes, Senator. I believe they were.

CHAIR: That is fine. I do not want to press the point any further than that.

BRANDIS: Do you know, Commander Banks? Do you know if they were?

BANKS: No, I do not. I have not interviewed any of them.

There is a loud gunshot upstage, and a fire alarm begins ringing loudly.

FAULKNER: The fire alarm is ringing. What would that mean on a ship, Commander? Time to jump overboard?

BANKS: I am not going to make any comment on the use of that word whatsoever!

CHAIR: We were going to break for morning tea at 11:30. Will you be much longer, Senator Faulkner?

FAULKNER: It might take me until about 12 o'clock. How does that sound?

CHAIR: In which case, I think we will break now for 10 minutes. Congratulations, Commander, you now have the dubious record of being the longest single witness before a Senate Inquiry!

FAULKNER: It could be worse, Commander, you could be a senator! Proceedings suspended from 11:40 a.m. to 11:52 a.m.

The SENATORS *have a brief tea break, chatting quietly amongst themselves as they have a cup of tea and biscuits.*

ACT 2: 'EVIL PEOPLE ENGAGED IN CHILD ABUSE'

CHAIR: I declare open this meeting of the Senate Select Committee on a Certain Maritime Incident. The remarks I am about to make you have heard 100 times. The committee has authorised the broadcasting of the public aspects of proceedings. The hearing will last until around 11 o'clock tonight and will resume at 9 a.m. tomorrow. The committee has agreed that it will hear from Rear Admiral Smith this evening. I'd like to pass on apologies from Senator Murphy, who will not be with us again this evening. Also, despite the rumours, Brad Pitt will not be playing the part of Senator Mason. Witnesses are reminded that the evidence given to the committee is protected by parliamentary privilege. It is important for witnesses to be aware that the giving of false or misleading evidence to the committee may constitute a contempt of the Senate. The committee is obliged to draw to the attention of a person any evidence which, in the committee's view, reflects adversely on that person, and to offer that person an opportunity to respond. Before I open, we are scheduled to finish at 11 tonight. That does not mean to say we have to go through until that hour. It could be that everyone will be so focused tonight that we could rise a lot earlier. I am sure that would make the support staff in this building, not to mention the witnesses and the rest of us, quite happy. I do urge the committee to be direct with their questions and see if we can come in under the hour set. Senator Collins.

COLLINS: Thank you, Mr Chair. Rear Admiral Smith, do you care to put a position to us about whether you believe that the abuse of children is a systematic pattern amongst asylum seekers?

SMITH [Deborah]: The use of children as a means of intimidating the boarding parties—the sailors and the soldiers—is one of the techniques being used by these people in an attempt to achieve their aim. Children were used by some people, and not all, as a means of applying moral pressure on our people. That was designed to appeal to our moral values. That was designed to strengthen their position and weaken our own and invite us to not persevere with the mission that we had been given. I think it is frankly a credit to the young men and women involved in this that they were able to persevere with their mission in the face of that.

CHAIR: I heard you say that when you originally said it, but could I just be clear about the language here—'The threat of doing so was an attempt to deal with our moral values'. We are talking about the threat, not an actuality?

SMITH: It is the threat of doing that. In our situation, if you take a sailor and he sees a mother and a child in distress, his natural inclination will be to help. That natural inclination, the culture of which we are a part, was being exploited.

COLLINS: Do you believe that that is not part of their own culture?

SMITH: In what respect?

COLLINS: The care of children. Do you think that there is a difference between our culture and their culture?

SMITH: I am not prepared to comment on the culture of the people involved here. I can only comment on our own culture and our own values. I saw our culture and our values, the things for which we stand, being exploited.

COLLINS: But such threats occur within our own society, our own culture, don't they?

SMITH: That could be true.

COLLINS: We hear about family law matters all the time where children are not only threatened but also actually harmed or killed within our own society, our own culture. Vice-Admiral Shackleton was very cautious about referring to moral blackmail, and I noticed in your discussion you also did not resort to that language. Do you care to comment?

SMITH: Without delving into the semantics of words here, at the end, I have no doubt at all that the behaviour of these people, was designed deliberately to place enormous pressure on professional young men and women who were being asked to do a very difficult job. That pressure was being applied with the sole purpose of undermining their professionalism and determination to achieve the mission that they had been given. Of that I have no doubt.

COLLINS: That concludes my questions, thank you, Chair.

CHAIR: Thank you, Senator Collins. Senator Brandis.

BRANDIS: There has been a lot of discussion about a pattern of conduct or a *modus operandi* during Operation Relex. [*Holding up a document*] I'd like to take you to this document…

COLLINS: Has this been tabled?

BRANDIS: I'm tabling it now. In it you will find a joint statement, in which all six officers or crewmen appear to share where they report:

MASON [David]: 'During the time that the TSE—'

STEPHEN: Transit Security Element.

MASON: '—was embarked, there were a few incidents of threats against children. During the riots self-harm and threats to children became commonplace and were not seen to be out of the ordinary—almost a "modus operandi". '

BRANDIS: A *modus operandi*. Do you see that?

SMITH: Yes.

BRANDIS: Thank you. I will just take you quickly through relevant parts of the statements to which I wish to draw attention. Do you see Incident Two at the top?

SMITH: Yes, I do.

BRANDIS: I just want to direct your attention to towards the end of paragraph five of Able Seaman Newham's statement where he reports:

MASON: 'I saw a solidly built male PII—'

DANIELLE: Potential Illegal Immigrant.

MASON: '—of about 40 years of age threaten to throw a child overboard on the port side. The TSE de-escalated the situation and the male calmed down and sat down.'

SMITH: Yes, that is what it states.

BRANDIS: Is that part of a pattern of conduct?

SMITH: Yes.

BRANDIS: Halfway down paragraph five it says:

MASON: 'I noticed a large Middle-Eastern-looking male leaning over the port guardrail with his arms fully extended holding an infant over the side of the vessel.'

BRANDIS: If a large man was leaning over the side of the guardrail with his arms fully extended, that is not really a very ambiguous set of circumstances, is it? It is not as if he is holding the child in the air near the guardrail.

SMITH: No, it is not. It is very clear.

BRANDIS: It says:

MASON: 'It appeared to me that he was threatening to throw the infant overboard. I was later informed by members of TSE that he had tried to throw the infant overboard but was unsuccessful as TSE prevented him from doing so, and the infant was brought safely back inboard.'

BRANDIS: See that? Part of the pattern of conduct?

SMITH: That is what the statement says and that is consistent with the pattern of behaviour.

CHAIR: You appreciate, Senator Brandis, that if this were a court of law that would be hearsay evidence, wouldn't it?

BRANDIS: A lot of this evidence is hearsay and, Senator Cook, often hearsay evidence is admissible—certainly if it is the best evidence available. As you have been at pains to remind me, Senator Cook, it is not a court.

The CHAIR *places a slide on the overhead projector. It reads:*

IS HEARSAY NARRATION OR RECOLLECTION?

CHAIR: That is right. I wish we could move quicker—we are appearing to be a court.

SENATOR BRANDIS *turns off the overhead projector.*

FAULKNER [Chris]: I am interested—and I have no objection to the terminology 'pattern of behaviour'; it is as good a use of words as any. It is a reasonably economical use of the English language, so I will go along with that. But the pattern of behaviour seems to matter an awful lot on the first weekend of the election campaign when Mr Costello is about to go on a Sunday television program and for the rest of the election campaign does not appear to have a great deal of significance at all.

SMITH: I do not think I will comment on that, Senator.

BRANDIS: Do you see a practical difference between throwing a young child into the sea and sabotaging a vessel on which a young child is being carried so that it sinks and the child ends up in the sea? Do you see a difference?

SMITH: I guess you are asking for my opinion there, Senator. The end result is exactly the same.

CHAIR: Do you make a distinction between a threat as opposed to an actual event? If it is oranges with oranges, it is throwing kids into the sea or sinking a vessel which kids are in—or if it is a threat to do either. They are direct comparisons in either case. But a threat to throw someone in is not the same as actually sinking a vessel, is it?

SMITH: That would be my view, yes.

BRANDIS: If the vessel is deliberately sunk and the children end up in the sea then they are actually in the sea; they are not merely being used as a lever or a device.

SMITH: As Senator Cook pointed out, trying to get apples and apples here, I would liken the deliberate sinking of the vessel to be the same as actually throwing someone in the water.

BRANDIS: Thank you.

BARTLETT: Before I start my questions—I could have raised this point at the time but I did not want to be seen to be trying to interrupt. Mr Chair, you mentioned before that people named adversely would be given the opportunity to respond. Can I clarify that that means the people on the various boats will get an opportunity to answer the allegations that were outlined today and the assertions that were made about their being evil people who engage in child abuse, moral blackmail and the like? It is a bit difficult when they are all locked away in a foreign land somewhere.

CHAIR: Outside of our jurisdiction—it is a bit difficult but, as I interpret the terms of reference, that is a relevant line of inquiry and we should apply our minds to how we conduct it.

MASON: Mr Chair, I do not recall anybody referring to them as 'evil people'. Do you?

BARTLETT: I do.

COLLINS: Yes, I do, Senator.

BRANDIS: I think I did say that the conduct reported was evil.

MASON: If you heard them talk about evil people then perhaps you can repeat it.

BARTLETT: Certainly I know the words 'moral blackmail' were used. Perhaps you can make a judgment and report about whether they should be condemned to hell, if that fits our terms of reference. A few of the statements also refer to the fact that people on board were either calling out for the UN—the United Nations—wanting to speak to the UN, or were stating that they were refugees. Is that of any relevance, in terms of the orders you had been given in the guidelines for the operations? Is the fact that people say, 'We are refugees' of any relevance?

SMITH: It had no relevance for us. Our mission was clear—that is, to intercept and then to carry out whatever direction we were given subsequent to that. The status of these people was irrelevant to us.

BARTLETT: Was that specifically outlined in the operational guidelines that you were given—that, when you have people in Australian territorial waters saying, 'I'm a refugee', such claims have no impact on your mission?

SMITH: Our mission was clear. Claims from the UAs were not factors to be taken into account in terms of how we conducted that mission. We expected those sorts of claims to be made. Our mission, however, was clear, and that is the way we executed it.

BARTLETT: That is the mission as given to you by our government.

SMITH: That is correct.

CHAIR: I am going to go to another subject, which will be my last subject. I want to get this clear—it is very clear to me but it seems to have been lost in the murk. If a child is thrown overboard, you would rescue it; if an adult jumps overboard you would rescue them. If you are a refugee, you do not need to throw a child overboard to cause the Navy to rescue someone overboard—an adult would equally serve that purpose if you were trying to create an incident such as that, wouldn't it?

SMITH: Your assumption is correct in the sense that it would not matter who went over the side, we would have a responsibility to rescue them. I guess you would need to talk to these individuals to see what their motives are for what they do. We certainly interpret what they do as applying pressure to our people.

CHAIR: At the level of threat. But at the level of actuality an adult jumping into the sea has the same effect in terms of what action it evokes from you.

SMITH: It has the same effect in what action it takes from us. It has less of an impact in the sense that an adult is able to look after themselves and a child is a child and that appeals to a certain part of our character that is different.

CHAIR: Yes. I am not in any way trying to excuse it. But an adult from the Middle East may not be an efficient swimmer. That may mean that they are at risk in any case—a lot of them.

BRANDIS: How does he know what the swimming ability of people from the Middle East is?

CHAIR: Because they do not have access.

FAULKNER: I think you are right, Admiral.

CHAIR: It is one of the cultural differences, for God's sake.

STEPHEN: Didn't you see the last Olympics?

DANIELLE: That was not in the transcript.

FAULKNER: The way I work it out, there are 2,215 asylum seekers listed on your spreadsheet. Would that be the correct figure? I have had a lot of time on my hands here. I have added it up three times on the calculator, so I am pretty confident. It sounds about right, doesn't it?

SMITH: It sounds about right, Senator.

FAULKNER: I reckon it is spot-on. Of those 2,215, we have come to the grand total of one being dropped over the side.

SMITH: One child?

FAULKNER: Well, one, which was a child.

SMITH: One child dropped over the side; that is correct.

FAULKNER: One child and no adults.

SMITH: There are many adults who have gone over the side.

FAULKNER: But they were not assisted.

SMITH: I have no evidence to suggest that any adult has been thrown over the side.

FAULKNER: That is right. So there were 2,215 and one was dropped over the side. And it was actually dropped or lowered; it was not thrown. Is that correct?

SMITH: 'Dropped' is the word being used in the statements, yes.

CHAIR: Thank you, Senator Faulkner… Hey, weren't you Senator Collins before?

CHRIS: It was the glasses. Collins, Faulkner, Faulkner, Collins.

CHAIR: Can we leave it there? Thank you very much, Rear Admiral Smith. It has been a long and, I hope, not too arduous…

BRANDIS: Was it longer than for Commander Banks?

CHAIR: I do not know.

BRANDIS: It was nine hours for Banks.

CHAIR: I have given up record keeping. On behalf of the committee, thank you very much, Rear Admiral. Committee adjourned at 11:18 p.m.

ACT 3: CHINESE WHISPERS AND 'TEAROOM GOSSIP'

The acting SENATORS *perform a series of phone calls. The calls overlap, and there is much chaos and confusion, with the continual sound of ringing telephones.*

STEPHEN: Hello, this is Andre, is that Mr Reith? Mr Peter Reith? Oh no, that is okay. Can you take a message for your papa? Just let him know that Andre, his offshore investment advisor phoned, about his shares in Chilton Corporation. That's right, Chilton Corporation. Yes. There was a shareholders' meeting in Adelaide today, and they voted to sack the board of directors. So if you could let him know, the Chilton board's been overthrown. *Au revoir.*

DEBORAH: Banks, it's Silverstone.

DAVID: Yes, Brigadier. Vessel disabled steering. Seven to eight nautical miles south. SUNCs threaten mass exodus. Man overboard. Child in the water.

DEBORAH: How old is the child?

DAVID: Five, six or seven. I cannot tell properly.

DEBORAH: Are they wearing life jackets?

DAVID: Yes, but some of the men have discarded theirs.

DEBORAH: Have you recovered all the PIIs?

DAVID: To the best of my knowledge we've got everyone.

DEBORAH: And that's exactly what you said, Banks. I wrote it down.

DAVID: With all due respect, sir, my recollection of the conversation is somewhat different. I made no mention of children.

NIKKI: I'm just trying to put together the pieces of the puzzle. How many did you say there went into the water? Five, six or seven? Seven. Could you email me the photos? I'd love to have a look at some video, yes. I don't know what the problem is. We need someone to look at it. It's not that hard, is it?

CHRIS: Hello, Chris here. Yes, I'm at The Performance Space. I just rang myself on my own phone. No, it's confirmed. Uh-huh. Yes, he was in the room when Smith got the call. Yes. The towel heads are throwing their children overboard.

DEBORAH *tells the children overboard story in Bahasa Indonesian.* CHRIS *tries to take her phone.*

DANIELLE: Yes, yes. Man believed to be sleeper agent of Osama bin Laden. He threatened to throw his child overboard if he couldn't cook his own food? What is this?

DAVID: No, I don't recall precisely what Brigadier Silverstone told me, but I imagine I would have passed on more or less exactly what I was told by him. Yes, and after that I went to the races. It was Sunday, and it was the Canberra Cup.

CHRIS: I don't care. That's an explanation, not a fuckin' excuse. Email, snail mail, courier. I need it here now. Look, put your blue suede shoes on and just do it!

NIKKI: Yes, he's a seven-year-old, and this will be his first swimming lesson.

DANIELLE: What's going on? We've been waiting for that food for hours. We're starving and we need to eat. I don't know, I didn't place the order, one of my staffers did. I don't know, five, six or seven supremes!

DEBORAH: Five, six, seven, eight? I don't know. It wasn't a toddler; it was an eight-year-old. Yes, I know an eight-year-old is heavy to hold over the guardrail, that's why they dropped it. Just write it down.

DAVID: This sequence of telephone calls begins at 0917 Canberra time. Just trying to put together the pieces of the puzzle.

STEPHEN: Right, mate, listen to me. Now this is important. Write this down. There's a sale on at Q. Kids tops and that. Mostly jumpers.

NIKKI: Yeah, I know it's Sunday. You're doing lamb? Lovely. Look, all hell's broken out here, and I won't be able to make it for lunch.

Look, you don't understand; I'm the Head of the Department. Don't give me that bit about being just like my father. Yes, Mum. Cold cuts will be fine. 'Bye.

DANIELLE: How does it look? Low-grade, low-quality? Look, look, look, we'd better not see the video then.

STEPHEN: Yeah, mate, I've got a quote for that you can use in your speech. It's from Winston Churchill. 'A lie gets halfway around the world before the truth has the chance to put its pants on.'

DAVID: Hello, Strategic Command? Yes, I've checked with Silverstone, and Banks, and it's an absolute fact, there were no children thrown overboard. Yes, I've checked the photos; they're of another event. And the video is inconclusive. Yes. Yes, I'll pass that on. Thank you, sir.

DEBORAH: Hi, Snookums, it's Puppy. Yeah, I've got shore leave. About fourteen hours. Can you pick me up at four? Yeah, I'll call you back.

NIKKI: Hello, I'd like a dozen red roses please. And a card. And it needs to be reasonably big card. And the inscription should read: 'Rough hew them as you will, though this be madness, there is method in it.' Yes, method. 'I must be cruel to be kind.' Signed: 'With sympathy, the Department.'

DANIELLE: I'm just looking at this place in Baxter, and it looks great. It's got a poolroom, a dining room, a playground, videos, the rooms look comfortable. The pictures are great. Be a great place for a holiday. What do you think?

STEPHEN: Hello, Ministry for the Arts? Yeah, I've got a great idea for a show. 2,200 pages of *Hansard*. Absolutely no dramatic climax, absolutely no children overboard, well, maybe one. Aright. Alright. Alright, I'll phone the Australia Council.

DAVID: Hello, it's Commander Banks here. The telephone doesn't normally ring that much, but during SIEV 4 it seemed to ring a bit more often than usual. I took the conversation in my towel. I was surprised. When the lady concerned introduced herself, I thought she said that she was a staff researcher. She might have said she was a staff reporter. She asked me a few quick questions, and I answered those questions truthfully. I also mentioned that we had photographs of what we had done. On the sage advice of my XO, who said, 'You might want to think twice about the photographs',

I did think twice about the photographs, and decided that sending photographs to Channel Ten was probably not a good career move. The thing that annoys me about all of this is that at no point did anybody call me back to ask for the information.

CHRIS: Hello, Embassy Jakarta? Oh, the Federal Police are there too. It's a party line! Look, I've got one question—how can we interfere with the boats somehow? See, they're all carrying money, jewels, heirlooms—how come they're not attacked by pirates more often? How can we interfere with the boats somehow? Ha, ha, ha. Well, you think of something. Yes, I know you're a policeman not a politician. Yes, I have ethics and morals too, you know. Look, I'm a member of Amnesty International. I was just joking. Ha, ha, ha. Look, I'm a very funny man.

DEBORAH: [*sobbing*] No, it wasn't my fault. Yes, I know it was my email. I didn't… I've got a mortgage! Alright, I'll hold.

Music begins. Enter JANE HALTON. *She leads the* SENATORS *in an aerobics routine.*

DEBORAH *places an overhead slide reading:*

THE ACTORS DID NOT UNANIMOUSLY AGREE WITH THE STAGING OF THIS SCENE. THEY USE A DEMOCRATIC MODEL TO CREATE THEATRE AND COMPROMISE IS A WORKING SOLUTION.

FAULKNER: [*cutting the music*] Ms Halton, have you given any thought as to whether you crossed the line from what might be reasonable activity as a bureaucrat, and in fact progressed your role in a way that could only be seen as a political tool of the Government? Have you given that any thought, Ms Halton?

HALTON [Nikki]: My view, categorically, is we behaved professionally and properly. I have a great deal of respect for the work that the people from the various departments put in on this issue. It is unfortunate that people have sought to portray humble servants of the public, which is what professional bureaucrats basically are, as being something other than they are.

CHAIR: Yes, but whichever way you want to cut it we are still stuck with this problem: news that kids were thrown overboard travelled at the speed of political light; the rejoinder that they were not thrown overboard did not even reach the Prime Minister after a month. That is the problem.

HALTON: I know you feel—

CHAIR: And everyone builds an edifice of proof that the first accusation did not have to meet but that the retraction does.

HALTON: This will come down inevitably to individual opinion.

CHAIR: It may, or it may come down to a better understanding of the facts.

HALTON: From my understanding of the facts, I describe this as being a bit like the parable of the blind man and the elephant. Are you familiar with it?

CHAIR: I am not sure at this hour that I want to become familiar with it—but I am pretty sure you are about to tell me.

HALTON: I am sorry, I am. You're blind. You walk up and you clasp onto something which feels like it is long and thin and leathery—and I am not going where you think I am—and what you have actually got hold of is the tail. You do not know, even though you can describe that bit of the tail in graphic detail, what the rest of the elephant looks like.

CHAIR: The problem with that analogy is that you have the helicopter view of the elephant.

HALTON: If you are blind, I suspect you cannot fly a helicopter—and, anyway, we should stop with parables at this hour of the evening—but we did not have the helicopter view. That is where I would dispute with you, because essentially we only saw what we were given from line agencies. The Department of the Prime Minister and Cabinet is not a line agency.

CHAIR: Yes, I accept that part of it. But nor did you seek to find other information out either.

HALTON: You only seek to find information when you have a doubt.

CHAIR: My position is—you say that refugees wearing life jackets is interesting and a new level of escalation in this operation, but that throwing children overboard is not a new pattern of threatening behaviour and therefore not requiring of investigation.

HALTON: What I said was: we thought that life jackets might be indicative of an intention to sink the vessel. That was the escalation we were expecting. Life jackets are neither here nor there; it is what you do with them and, as we suspected and as we all know, that vessel was sunk.

CHAIR: Yes, but the fact that children were being thrown overboard—as the report you had—does not appear to you to be a new pattern of behaviour worthy of further investigation? That is my whole problem with the evidence.

HALTON: The answer to that is no. Had that been an issue raised, or particularly germane to anything in terms of operational detail, we may well have pursued it. At the time it did not seem that that was the case, and that was where the issue rested.

CHAIR: So the report got broadcast but no-one bothered to find out anything more because it was not convenient?

HALTON: No. And that is a misrepresentation, Senator. You are implying that an active decision was made not to do something because of convenience. The reality is we did seek information.

CHAIR: And you got it; that is the evidence.

HALTON: Can I tell you that there was no point in this process that the advice that was given was couched in any notion of convenience? The information was, if I use the old bureaucratic standard, frank and fearless based on the facts as we knew them, based on our technical and professional advice. That is absolutely an accurate reflection of the truth.

CHAIR: So how do you explain it, then, that it works one way but it does not work the other way? It works with the first advice, but it does not work with the second advice. Isn't that a systemic failure? We are sitting exactly in your seat. We have the commander of the ship saying that as soon as he became aware of the misrepresentation he corrected it.

HALTON: I am aware of that, Senator.

CHAIR: And we had Brigadier Silverstone saying exactly the same. We went right up the line and they all said that they corrected it. The line peaks with you.

HALTON: But they did not correct it to me. The reality is that…

CHAIR: So they are wrong? We should call them back.

HALTON: No, Senator. Not one of those people, as I understand it, has given you evidence that they came and corrected it to the task force. I never had a conversation with Commander Banks; I never had a conversation with Silverstone or Smith or, can I say, Vice-Admiral Shackleton.

CHAIR: And we are expected to believe that the most hands-on Prime Minister, in election campaigning, takes the front page of the newspapers around Australia essentially the day or the second day after he announces an election and never asks another question again about the issue that got him favourable front-page coverage?

HALTON: I cannot make any comment about what the Prime Minister did or did not ask. Going back to my elephant, what I know is that I was never asked and the task force was never asked and, indeed, we never had any reason to ask.

Sleazy music begins. JANE HALTON *and* SENATOR COOK *get closer and closer together.*

CHAIR: I have no doubt that everyone worked very hard, but I have some doubt in believing that this is an example of sterling professionalism by the Public Service.

An overhead slide reads:

JANE HALTON DID NOT HAVE SEX WITH SENATOR COOK. SHE WAS HOWEVER AN AEROBICS INSTRUCTOR.

HALTON: I cannot comment on that, Senator. I can just tell you what I know. Now that I am tired, and we are all tired, let us take the emotional language out. If I have used that language before I regret it, so let us talk about the seeking of clarification and detail which was professionally what people were doing.

The SENATORS *begin to party. Champagne and pizza arrive and are consumed. A toast is made to 'professionalism'. The party quickly degenerates, with wild dancing and games that get quickly out of control. Midway through the party,* DANIELLE *stands on the table and speaks into the microphone, drink in hand.*

DANIELLE: Sunday. Rehearsal strategies. Pick a witness. Introduce yourself. Play with storytelling modes. Excuses, summaries and explanations. Try to make sense. Make it happy, make it sexy, make it boring, make it up. Translate it, riff on it, rip it up. Render it guttural and into gibberish. Make it a comedy. Make it a tragedy. Make it the hardest thing you've ever had to say. Experiment with delivery. Focus on bigness, weight, investment, subterfuge, lying, urgency. Enact

Chinese whispers with your stories, and when they come back to you it's like hearing them for the very first time.

The door slams and the music ends abruptly. The SENATORS *are caught out in the wreckage of the party.*

ACT 4: SUNK WITHOUT A TRACE

Enter MR TONY KEVIN, *a former diplomat.*

CHAIR: Mr Tony Kevin, speaking in a private capacity.

KEVIN [Chris]: Thank you, Mr Chair. If I could just read my statement. 'A boat left Bandar Lampung in southern Sumatra on 18 or 19 October, bound for Christmas Island, carrying over 400 people. This boat was grotesquely overloaded, under armed duress and probably also sabotaged. It sank on 19 October, drowning 353 people and leaving only 44 survivors. Coastwatch Australia knew from an intelligence source when this boat had left, where from, its likely speed, and that it was heading for Christmas Island. Coastwatch did not pass this information on. As a result, the Navy was not told about a grave safety of life at sea situation that was taking place only 150 nautical miles north of the nearest Navy ship, the frigate HMAS *Arunta*. But *Arunta* was not told, Operation Relex was not told, Jane Halton's People Smuggling Taskforce was not told until three days after the boat had sunk. Why was information about departure of a Suspected Illegal Entry Vessel, which Coastwatch clearly had, not given to Operation Relex and the Navy until far too late to save lives? How could this be possible at a time when the Australian Government was giving top priority to its tough new border protection exercise? An argument of administrative error is not credible. In almost every case of these Suspected Illegal Entry Vessels coming down, we knew they were coming and that information was based on intelligence material. So I do not think it is conjecture to say that there is something very odd here. If this reporting was taken out of the information chain, this was done deliberately. The important thing is that the information was in Canberra and that it was mishandled in Canberra, with callous disregard for human life and with tragic consequences. There is clear public knowledge now that there was some Australian official foreknowledge of the circumstances that led to the deaths of these 65 men, 142 women, and 146 children. This cries out for explanation and accountability. I hope that senators might have had a chance to read the heart-rending accounts of survivors that were attached to my original submission. There are key issues at stake here both of human rights and justice and of the Australian Defence Force's integrity that need to be fearlessly investigated.'

BRANDIS: Mr Kevin, who are you suggesting sabotaged this vessel?

KEVIN: I am not suggesting anything at this point. I am just setting out the known facts about the departure, the sinking and the rescue, and saying it creates a very great puzzle.

MASON: Mr Kevin, it is just that all the other evidence of sabotage that we have had has been sabotage by the unauthorised arrivals.

FAULKNER [Deborah]: I think these events are, as you say, extraordinarily tragic. I am concerned to hear what you have said about sabotage. If there are any other concerns that you have or light you can throw onto this, I would appreciate your doing so.

KEVIN: Senator, without making any allegations or accusations, I want to say that the context and the timing of this sinking were enormously useful for the Australian border protection operation. Consider the chronology: until this time, there had been a number of Suspected Illegal Entry Vessels coming down, six in all. In all of those cases, the strategy of repelling asylum-seeker boats had not succeeded. The Government has recently been congratulating itself on how successful it has been in halting the flow of people smuggling, and it mentions a number of reasons for that, but I would suggest perhaps the most important reason was this terrible tragedy.

FAULKNER: I want to be clear on this. You are not suggesting any possible Australian involvement, in what you describe as the probable sabotage?

BRANDIS: I am itching to understand what are you saying, Mr Kevin. You directed us to page 461 of *Hansard* of this committee where Rear Admiral Smith tells us:

MASON: 'We'—

BRANDIS: That is the Navy—

MASON: —'had some information that a boat might have been being prepared in the vicinity of Sunda Strait but we had no real fixed information as to when it was going to sail.'

KEVIN: Senator, I am not here to make allegations; I am here to bring to your committee's attention discrepancies in the public record of what Australia knew about this boat and what it did with the information. A system of intelligence, surveillance and interception that worked very well in the case of every other Suspected Illegal Entry Vessel failed to work in this case and 353 people died.

MASON: Do I understand you to be telling me that you do not allege any Australian culpability in these deaths?

KEVIN: I am not here to allege; I am here to bring discrepancies on the public record regarding the Australian system of information and command to your attention, for your committee to do what you wish to do with it.

BRANDIS: Perhaps Senator Faulkner, Senator Mason and I are all stupid, but it is not apparent to us that there are such discrepancies in the public record.

FAULKNER: I wish you would not include me in that group.

BRANDIS: In any event, Mr Kevin, you do not suggest there is a culpability. Is that what I take from your evidence? At the end of the day, you do not make an allegation to that effect.

KEVIN: Senator, I am not in a position to say whether there is culpability or not. It is for your committee to find this out.

MASON: And it is for you, is it, to leave the slur on the honour and competency of the Royal Australian Navy and the Australian Defence Force in general on the basis of no evidence at all?

KEVIN *is pushed off the stage by the conference table as* BRANDIS *speaks.*

KEVIN: No, it is for me to say that this public record shows that the information in the command system was not working as it should have been in this very important case and 353 people died.

BRANDIS: Is there any other piece of evidence to which you wish to direct us?

FAULKNER: Mr Kevin, how did you become involved or develop an interest in this particular incident? As I said before, it is a horrific tragedy and it is understandable that anyone would take a close interest in it, but you have taken a particularly close interest in it. Do not read into that that I am critical in any way, because I am not. I am pleased that an Australian citizen would take such a close interest in something like this. How did it develop?

DANIELLE: [*reading*] 'I boarded the boat with 15 other family members— nine drowned and six remained. We clung on to a plank of timber for 20 hours drifting in the water. Something I witnessed left a very strange impression, a baby with its umbilical cord still attached to the mother was amongst those who drowned. There was 150 children on board, only 4 survived.' The man broke down and could not continue his account.

The actors begin to clear away all evidence of the performance. The table is cleaned and used as a slab. STEPHEN's *naked body is cleaned and prepared for the mortuary.*

COMPUTERISED VOICE: [*reading*] The bottom level of the boat had women and children, the middle level had families and the top level had men only. No-one survived from the bottom level, as the boat capsized people were trapped with little air, I was inside with the children, there remained a small area where air was trapped, I had a life jacket and was able to swim to safety, but the others, the children and the women had no chance. Fish were biting at our bodies, I had to be hospitalised due to fish bites. This horrible scene, between the broken boat, the fish biting at us and the dead bodies. If suicide was permitted, I am certain many would have let go. I appeal to every person with humanity, I appeal to the Australian people. When they came to us and showed us the boat, we were told that this boat was not the one to get us to Australia, it was only a transit boat that would get us to the boat that would bring us to Australia, they put us in a very small place on the boat, with children on top of each other, we remained there till 6:00 a.m. and then the boat moved out and kept moving till 3:10 p.m. when it began to sink. The engine stopped working, some went to fix the engine whilst others were taking water out and a third group trying to move left and right to keep the boat balanced in the water. The water came from the left and then the right and the boat capsized. When it did, the women and the children started to come out, I grabbed my daughters, aged five and two, my husband was fixing the engine inside, my daughter was crying, wanting her father, her father came out to see them before the boat capsized and then went back to fix the engine. As I was holding my daughters, trying to keep them from drowning, a woman came and stepped on my elder daughter as she was scurrying for safety, I pulled my daughter up, the women kept tripping on my daughter repeatedly until my daughter sank and I could not pull her up anymore. I only had my younger daughter now, I started to look for my husband, I could not find my elder daughter anywhere. A woman, looking for her two daughters came, she did not know what she was doing, she pushed me and my daughter under water. I was able to keep holding my daughter, she pushed us a second time but we were still able to go up, on the third occasion, my daughter was lost. I saw another man wearing a life jacket, I asked him to help me find my daughter, as he turned, I found that it was my husband. I told him that my daughters were taken under, he said: maybe someone has rescued them, he was able to grab a floating plank of timber for me, we went on the plank for a while, I said that I am in despair for my daughters, he said maybe someone has rescued them. Then I saw my small daughter floating, eyes open, dead, her father embraced her and started calling her name, he kissed her and hugged her, I said: God has taken her, he said come see her; I said: I cannot look at her; he left her, then a little later, we saw the body of my elder daughter with the body of the woman who was responsible for her going under water, the other women's two daughters, twelve and eleven were also floating by her, both dead, my daughter was on top of her head. He said: I have lost my family, I have brought you to this, I do not deserve to live; he said: I cannot stay, I do not want to see you die in front of me. As he was talking, he was looking very tired, he was crying, his grip became loose because of his exhaustion, a wave then came and washed him away from the timber. His friend saw him drifting past, he asked him: Why did you leave your wife? He said: my wife died, I don't deserve to live; he was floating with life jacket, looking to the sky, saying: this is because of me, I brought my family to their death. He asked me to forgive him, he said: I brought you to Australia, you did not want to come here; I was left alone, the other survivors were taken elsewhere by the waves, I felt alone until the middle of the night, I heard cries from others from time to time, but I could not see them.

When we were brought to the boat, we were told that we would be transported to the main ship, we found this to be untrue. We felt like meat on meat, like sardines, my brother was sick, they put him on the top deck, we were all unwell, the boat moved. I saw a ten-month-old girl before the accident, she fell from her father's arms into the ocean, people were packed on top of each other, a small ship with people seasick and women and children afraid and crying. Then a crack appeared in the boat and water started to gush inside and the men could not keep up with the water trying to throw it outside with buckets. There were about 100 life jackets only, people were crying. The boat broke up within seconds, the waves washed the family members apart. I saw a woman giving birth in the ocean, I saw my brother being washed away by the waves, I called out to him but saw him crying. When night came, I saw a group of 22 young men with a thirteen-year-old girl and a lady who lost her three daughters, lost her son and lost her mother-in-law. My brother did not want to come to Australia, he only wanted to get us to safety and return. Thirst, hunger and salt water, people had not eaten since Wednesday so that they do not throw up, I clung onto a plank with another lady, all the water around us was contaminated with fuel, the little girl died from exhaustion and the cold, she did not have a life jacket, from our group of 25, there were only seven left. Time passed quickly, like a miracle, dawn came at what felt like 1:00 a.m., I prayed to God to take my life, I could no longer cope with the pain, we were then rescued by an Indonesian boat. There were two engines, one was not working, I was trying to repair it, it was an old engine but we repaired it as new, I never imagined that the boat would sink… I never imagined that the boat would sink… I never imagined that the boat would sink… I never imagined that the boat would sink… I never imagined that the boat would sink… I never imagined that the boat would sink… I never imagined that the boat would sink… I never imagined…

CHAIR: [*lying on the slab*] Senator Mason, Senator Brandis and Senator Faulkner have left, but that is meant as no disrespect to you. If they had not left, they would have missed their planes, and the end of the examination was in sight, so I pass on their regards and thank you for your appearance here. We do not have a listed date for another hearing—this may well be the last formal hearing of the inquiry.

I cannot be certain about that, because there are outstanding matters yet to be settled as well as other information that has been requested. There is also the possibility of other witnesses being called. On behalf of the committee, I pass on our thanks and appreciation. Committee adjourned at 6:45 p.m.

Slow fade to black.

THE END

The complete Senate Committee transcripts and reports can be found online at:
http://www.aph.gov.au/Parliamentary_Business/Committees/Senate_ Committee?url=maritime_incident_ctte/index.htm

THE **RAINBOW** DARK

VICTORIA CARLESS

Jan Nary as Gloria and Kaye Stevenson as Babs in the 2006 Metro Arts Theatre production of The Rainbow Dark, *in association with Backbone Youth Arts and Playlab, in Metro Arts Theatre, Brisbane. (Photo: Nick Martin.)*

Introduction

The catch cry of contemporary global anti-capitalism movements, 'another world is possible', can be mapped onto the decision made at the end of Victoria Carless's play by one of her 60-something protagonists, younger sister Babs. It is a decision to imagine another world and to do the unthinkable—disobey the government.

The Rainbow Dark won the Queensland Theatre Company's 2006 George Landen Dann award and premiered at Brisbane's Metro Arts Theatre the same year. In 2008, the play was performed at JUTE Theatre in Cairns. By scaling political manoeuvres down to the domestic sphere via the medium of satire, *The Rainbow Dark* crystallises the essentially banal attitudes and impulses that underpin the act of suspending another person's liberty. Among Babs's and her elder sister Gloria's chief characteristics is obedience, a deep-seated respect for and trust in the government; theirs isn't the obedience of brainwashed denizens of an authoritarian regime, but simply the kind of good sense that keeps civic society ticking over. This is what makes their behaviour so chilling: it is, on one level, entirely *reasonable*.

Carless's play, like version 1.0's *CMI (A Certain Maritime Incident)* (which is otherwise a very different play), doesn't dramatise a face-to-face encounter between Australians and asylum seekers; instead, plenty of words, of rationalisation and patriotic platitudes, obscure the question of what such an encounter might consist of. In its premier season in Brisbane, *The Rainbow Dark* was prefaced with an opening sound bite of John Howard's vilifying narration of the 'children overboard' affair (for a summary of this, see my introduction to *CMI*, p. 3), including the statement, 'I don't want people like that in Australia. Genuine refugees don't do that … They hang onto their children' (quoted in *Dark Victory* by Marr and Wilkinson, p. 251). These words are spoken from the same unstable moral high ground to which the sisters cling.

The tone of Carless's text is a curious mix of homely, comic banter between two fussy women, and a creeping mood of suffocation, of something being very wrong. Although it is set in the present, quaint references to being a 'Modern Woman', to suburban sewing rooms and to men who come courting, give the world of the play more than a tinge of insularity, or of being stuck. Kat Henry's 2006 production utilised the intimate space of the Metro Arts Theatre to heighten a sense of unchanging domestic order, where floral couches still covered in their protective plastic create contaminant-free zones.

The incarcerated 'Peoples From Elsewhere Who Don't Recognise Perfectly Good Borders' are represented in *The Rainbow Dark* only in snatches and traces: anxious discussions between Gloria and Babs, the occasional muffled cry, a baby's slipper. They exist in the play the same way they do for most Australians, that is, unseen and (occasionally) imagined. The play's gaze is turned on 'us', the citizens in whose interests immigration detention is implemented.

Gloria and Babs's 'appropriate vestibule' for containing their quota of 'Peoples from Elsewhere', the cupboard under their stairs, remains invisible to the audience for the duration of the play. It is invisible, yet it's all the sisters can think about (except of course, Gloria's prospective lover, Donald). In *The Poetics of Space* (1994, first published in French in 1958), Gaston Bachelard's lyrical reading of how we inhabit intimate domestic spaces, the philosopher considers the way cellars can represent the intensified emotional life of a house's inhabitants, becoming spaces associated with 'buried madness, walled in tragedy' (p. 20). While Gloria and Babs's cupboard isn't subterranean, it is beneath stairs, and may be read as the repository of their exaggerated fears.

The presence of the sisters' dog, the respectably named Sylvia, drives home *The Rainbow Dark*'s surreal and absurdist qualities. Sylvia's character description demands some nutting out by the actor: 'She is almost like an echo or a conscience. Her voice should reflect this. Only Babs can hear her'. This hulking, farting creature proves herself to be the most humane in the play. And yet, when we learn that even the staunch Gloria has secretly acted more benevolently towards the Peoples From Elsewhere than she or her government-issue handbook will officially allow, we realise that she knew all along that another world is possible.

Emma Cox

The Rainbow Dark was first produced by Metro Arts Theatre in association with Backbone Youth Arts and Playlab, as part of the *Fragments* season of short plays, at Metro Arts Theatre, Brisbane, on 25 October 2006, with the following cast:

GLORIA	Jan Nary
BABS	Kaye Stevenson
SYLVIA	Dirk Hoult
DONALD	Hugh Taylor

Director, Kat Henry

CHARACTERS

GLORIA, late 60s

BABS, mid 60s

SYLVIA, a dog. She is almost like an echo or a conscience. Her voice should reflect this. Only Babs can hear her.

DONALD, a butcher, early 60s, courting Gloria

SETTING

A living room / a kitchen / a cupboard under the stairs. Early evening.

PROLOGUE

In darkness. There is the sound of footsteps—those of GLORIA *and* SYLVIA. *The sound of the low cries of people incarcerated, muffled by a heavy door. The language is indistinguishable. The cries increase as the footsteps approach. The door is slowly opened.* SYLVIA *begins to bark. The sound of 'fear' rushes out. A tray of food is set down. Silence. The door closes slowly. Muffled sounds of desperate eating.*

SYLVIA: Woof, woof—window!
GLORIA: Quiet, Sylvia!
SYLVIA: Window, woof, window!

> *The cries increase.*

GLORIA: Sylvia! Stop that! You're encouraging them!
SYLVIA: Woof woof woof woof window!
GLORIA: Sylviaaaa!

> GLORIA *drags* SYLVIA *up the stairs.* SYLVIA *and the cries fade out.*

> ***

BABS *and* GLORIA *enter, to sit down to an evening cuppa. The tea things are assembled on a tray. They use fine bone china. There are three cups. The ladies lower themselves down onto their plastic covered couch. Much fussing. The floor is covered in plastic carpet runners.* SYLVIA *enters.*

GLORIA: Sit, Sylvia!

> SYLVIA *snuffles as she settles.*

That cursed dog. You really should have her put down.

> *Pause.*

BABS: Yes dear. Fancy a cuppa? Just a quick one. Before he arrives?
GLORIA: What a good idea. It'll settle my nerves.
BABS: Lovely. I'll just pop my teeth in.

> BABS *retrieves her teeth from a glass on the tea tray and pops them in her mouth. She pours the tea.*

49

Gloria, darling?

GLORIA: Yes pet?

BABS: Are these your teeth or mine?

GLORIA: Let me see.

> BABS *removes the teeth and hands them to* GLORIA. GLORIA *removes her own teeth and tries to fit them. A struggle. They do not fit.*

They're yours pet.

> GLORIA *hands them back to* BABS *who re-fits them—pop!*

BABS: Thank you dear.

> *Pause.*

One sugar, or two?

GLORIA: Two, dear. [*Pause.*] I don't know why you ask. I've been taking my tea the same way for fifty years. Sisters should come to know these things.

BABS: Yes, dear.

GLORIA: It's always been white with two sugars. Except of course when Teddy Hunt was courting. Then it was one. Watching my weight, you know.

BABS: Yes. Indeed. A lady must never appear to overindulge.

> *She takes a sip of her tea.*

GLORIA: Or slurp.

BABS: Yes pet. [*Pause.*] Gloria dear?

GLORIA: Yes pet?

BABS: Will you be having one sugar this evening, do you think?

GLORIA: Well that all depends on *him*, doesn't it?

> SYLVIA *yawns. Loudly.*

I honestly don't know why you encourage that dog inside Barbara. She smells so.

> SYLVIA *snorts.*

And she snores. We should dump her.

BABS: Yes my love.

> *Pause.*

GLORIA: Have you made the sandwiches?

BABS: Yes dear. Vegemite. And some jam ones for the children. They're in the fridge.

GLORIA: Good. We don't want any fuss while our guest is here. [*Pause.*] I hope you were economical.

BABS: Yes dear. Just a scraping of butter.

GLORIA: A smidgeon of Vegemite?

BABS: A speck of jam.

GLORIA: Good. We're not made of money you know.

BABS: I know dear.

GLORIA: Of course we get some assistance. Some benefits from the government. It's only a token, mind.

BABS: Of course dear.

GLORIA: Nothing really to speak of. Doesn't cover the cost. Not when you account for it. The risk we're taking.

BABS: That's very true dear.

GLORIA: Of course, it's our civic duty. Our responsibility. We're very civil-minded, wouldn't you say?

BABS: We are dear. Very civil-minded indeed. We don't shirk our duty.

GLORIA: Not everyone could do it, could they? Take on this type of responsibility. It's not for everyone.

BABS: No they couldn't. No indeed. We're a special two.

> *Pause.*

GLORIA: Take Helen from number three. She couldn't handle it. She only lasted two weeks. And she claims to be a Modern Woman! [*Pause.*] Or Mrs Robertson, from down the road. Couldn't hack it either. Gave it away after a month. Just gave them up—fancy! Imagine the bureaucratic headache! I think some of her lot are mixed in with ours now. [*Pause.*] And she had a *husband*.

BABS: They just couldn't take it, it seems. The thumps under the stairs. The cries in the night. [*Pause.*] The voices in the dark.

GLORIA: Don't think of that, Barbara. Don't speak of it. It's a minor inconvenience. Compared to the good we're doing.

BABS: [*reminding herself*] Yes, yes don't dwell. It's for the greater good.

> *There is a low muffled moan. They pause.* SYLVIA *barks. She looks at* BABS *and barks again.*

GLORIA: [*to* SYLVIA] Quiet!

BABS: Yes pet, settle down.

GLORIA: Besides, it won't be for too much longer now.

BABS: Yes, there will be a solution soon. A government action to address the issue.

GLORIA: A policy amendment.

BABS: A law.

GLORIA: A constitutional rectification.

BABS: A by-law.

> *A slightly louder muffled moan. They pause.* SYLVIA *barks then begins to whine. She sits up and begs.*

GLORIA: Quiet, Sylvia!

BABS: They always set her off.

GLORIA: She'll annoy the neighbours. They'll report us.

BABS: Oh dear—will they take her away?

GLORIA: Yes and pound her up.

BABS: She wouldn't be so fond of that.

GLORIA: It's probably the best thing. [*Pause.*] As I was saying, there'll be something done to maintain the agenda.

BABS: Yes, something significant will happen soon. [*Pause.*] How long has it been, exactly?

GLORIA: I'd say, at a guess, about twelve months.

BABS: About a year.

GLORIA: That's right, about twelve months.

BABS: We've had people living under our staircase for a year.

GLORIA: We've had Peoples From Elsewhere Who Don't Recognise Perfectly Good Borders, *temporarily* housed in an appropriate vestibule for approximately twelve months. Give or take a week.

BABS: We've had people living in the cupboard under our stairs for *one year*. Without even the window open.

> *There is a muffled cry, louder than before. Longer pause.* SYLVIA *whimpers but is cut short by a* look *from* GLORIA.

GLORIA: Speaking of which…

BABS: It must be just about time to feed them.

GLORIA: It's your turn, I believe. I did it last night.

> *Pause.*

BABS: How many are there, do you think?
GLORIA: I don't know. I never look.
BABS: Well, what did the booking sheet say?
GLORIA: I can't remember. Twenty. Or twenty-five.
BABS: There would be at least half a dozen children.
GLORIA: I never look.
BABS: At least six kids.
GLORIA: I don't look. Can't bear their eyes.

A louder muffled cry. Pause. SYLVIA *moves to* GLORIA*'s feet and begins to cough and retch. She is coughing something up. The sisters watch in horror as she coughs up what looks like a baby slipper.*

GLORIA: [*to herself*] Please, Sylvia, no.

SYLVIA *moves away from* GLORIA.

Sylvia! You wretched thing!
BABS: Sylvia! Naughty!

SYLVIA *hangs her head.*

What *is* it?
GLORIA: Nothing to speak of. She's been through the bins again.
BABS: It looks like a... *baby's slipper*—
GLORIA: Nonsense. Just a bit of fluff! We must clean it up! He'll be here in a minute. Take a look, would you?
BABS: Yes dear.

BABS *goes to the door to check.* GLORIA *picks the slipper up, holds it to her, and puts it in her pocket.* BABS *returns.*

He certainly is taking his time.
GLORIA: Donald is a busy man, Barbara. [*Pause.*] How do I look dear?
BABS: Just lovely pet. Peach is definitely your colour.
GLORIA: I have been told so, on occasion.
BABS: Although... you don't think...
GLORIA: What?
BABS: That it might be... a touch... just a tad...
GLORIA: Spit it out.
BABS: Inappropriate? A bit *forward*, even? After all, it is a negligee.
GLORIA: It's a *nightgown*. It *is* *night*-time.

BABS: Is there a difference? I was never certain.

GLORIA: Of course there's a difference.

BABS: But for a visitor… a *man*…

GLORIA: I don't know what you're worried about Barbara—it's completely lined. [*Pause.*] Besides, sometimes it serves the mature woman well to be *slightly* less than subtle…

BABS *considers her own outfit. She undoes her top button.*

BABS: How do *I* look?

GLORIA: Fine dear.

An even louder muffled cry. SYLVIA *howls.*

Sylvia, that's it!

BABS: I could almost swear that she's trying to tell us something.

GLORIA: Don't be absurd Barbara!

BABS: You don't think so?

GLORIA: I most certainly do not! I've had enough!

BABS: Gloria, please pet. [*Pause.*] After all, they are making quite a racket tonight.

GLORIA: She should close her ears to it. I do!

BABS: Yes dear. [*Pause.*] Tell me Gloria, do you think I've made enough?

GLORIA: Enough what?

BABS: Sandwiches. Do you think they get hungry?

GLORIA: What a ridiculous question!

The doorbell rings—a novelty ring tone. GLORIA *and* BABS *freeze, then fuss with the couch/room and their clothes.*

That's him! You get the door. Where should I sit?

BABS: Don't panic! [*She thinks. Pointing*] There—where the light is softest. And me?

GLORIA: [*pointing to a dimly lit area/the corner*] Over there.

The doorbell rings again—a novelty ring tone. They jump. GLORIA *takes her place, while* BABS *rises from the plastic-covered couch. She walks across the plastic carpet runner offstage to the front door. The sound of the front door opening.*

BABS: [*off*] Good evening, Donald! What a surprise! Gloria we have a visitor—Donald is here.

GLORIA: Come in, Donald!

> BABS *and* DONALD *enter. They walk down the plastic carpet runner and settle on the plastic-covered couch.*

Good evening, Donald. You'll have to excuse me, I look a fright in my night gown! If only I'd known you were coming—I would have dressed more appropriately! Do sit down!

DONALD: Good evening, ladies. [*Clearing his throat*] I've brought you some sausages.

GLORIA: Donald! How lovely! Thank you.

DONALD: No trouble at all. Plenty more where they came from.

GLORIA: They'll go nicely with some mash for tea. Of course, Barbara won't have any—she's a strict vegetarian. She doesn't eat meat of any kind. Babs, you'll have to put some spam out for yourself pet.

BABS: Yes dear.

DONALD: There are some nice bones for the dog as well.

GLORIA: That really wasn't necessary, Donald.

BABS: Thank you Donald, Sylvia will love them.

> SYLVIA *barks, trots up to* DONALD, *sniffs his pockets.*

GLORIA: No, Sylvia! Do not sniff! Down!

DONALD: It's fine, I—

GLORIA: Down, Sylvia! That's enough! Out!

> SYLVIA *exits, tail between her legs.*

BABS: She could smell the bones.

DONALD: What a nice puppy.

GLORIA: I apologise, Donald, for my sister's unsavoury dog. I have told her time and again, no good comes of taking in strays. No good at all!

BABS: She's quite a dear dog really…

DONALD: Seems harmless to me.

GLORIA: I've told her before Donald, you know what they say—'soft heart, soft head'.

DONALD: I have to confess I'm a bit of a softie meself, when it comes to animals…

GLORIA: Nonsense, a butcher! A strapping man of meat like you!

DONALD: Gloria, you're embarrassing me—

GLORIA: [*giggling girlishly*] Oh, Donald! And so to what do we owe the pleasure of your company this evening?

DONALD: No special reason—I was just in the neighbourhood and I thought I might call in…

GLORIA: Babs mentioned you were about.

DONALD: Yes I just dropped in on number three—she's quite the modern woman, you know.

GLORIA: Yes. So we've heard.

DONALD: But I do enjoy coming here. And how are you two, my dears?

GLORIA: We're fine Donald. Couldn't be better.

BABS: We're well. Really quite good.

DONALD: And what about… how are things with the… the um… *arrangement*?

GLORIA: Wonderful. No problems at all. None whatsoever.

BABS: Yes, everything's peachy.

Pause.

DONALD: Good. Glad to hear it. I'm relieved, in fact. [*Pause.*] Truth be told, I was worried. You ladies have taken on quite a responsibility. A burden, one might say. And I thought, maybe with all the unrest—the recent escapes and whatnot—I thought you might be having a hard time of it… what with your… charges… and all.

GLORIA: Nonsense. Not at all.

BABS: Everything's just super.

Pause.

GLORIA: Pardon, Donald, did you say unrest?

BABS: You mentioned escapes?

DONALD: You haven't heard?

GLORIA: Heard what, exactly?

DONALD: It was on the news this morning. Two Peoples From Elsewhere Who Don't Recognise Perfectly Good Borders have escaped, from a sewing room in Marraborne.

GLORIA: How unfortunate!

DONALD: It said in the paper that the lock to the room was cut by pinking shears.

BABS: That sounds like an inside job to me…

DONALD: Mrs Feathersworth—the woman who owned the sewing room, has been taken in for questioning.

BABS: Poor Mrs Feathersworth!

DONALD: They are saying that it may affect government Peoples From Elsewhere Who Don't Recognise Perfectly Good Borders policy—

GLORIA: Of course it will affect the policy! Ninnies like that Feathersworth woman shouldn't be given such responsibility!

DONALD: The government are desperate Gloria, what with the major centres being overloaded. I suppose they have to take what they can get—

GLORIA: How that woman passed the screening test, I'll never know. Surplus Peoples are only to be detained in suitable residential civilian properties. It's in the handbook! Page one!

BABS: You don't think Mrs Feathersworth had anything—

GLORIA: Of course not! It was obviously someone sympathetic to their cause—a bleeding heart who cut the lock for a warm fuzzy!

BABS: But the pinking shears… perhaps it was planned.

DONALD: These things often are…

GLORIA: Nonsense! They escaped of their own accord. She was only doing her duty. Albeit incompetently!

BABS: Her civil responsibility. Bungling non-withstanding.

GLORIA: And for what—ingratitude!

BABS: Obviously some people just don't know a good sewing room when they see one.

GLORIA: Still, nothing for us to worry about. We're safe here.

BABS: No need to fret. Our locks are strong. And there are no pinking shears to speak of.

GLORIA: I'd say it's just a base attempt at federal scare mongering.

BABS: Really just an example of departmental scapegoating. [*Pause.*] What will happen to them, do you think? The Peoples From Elsewhere Who Don't Recognise Perfectly Good Borders?

GLORIA: Don't even consider it, Barbara! It's not our concern.

    Pause.

DONALD: Well it's good that you're taking it so well. I was afraid… It's just… I wouldn't want anything to happen to you Gloria—to either of you, I mean…

GLORIA: That's sweet! Isn't that sweet, Babs pet? Donald was worried about us!

BABS: It's sweet, yes.

GLORIA: But you needn't worry. We're perfectly capable.

BABS: We're managing quite well.

GLORIA: Now let us hear no more on the matter. How is business, Donald?

DONALD: As well as to be expected, Gloria.

GLORIA: Whatever do you mean?

DONALD: Admittedly, things have been quiet. A lot of my customers are feeling the strain, what with all the extra mouths to feed. Let's just say, roast beef isn't at the top of their shopping list.

GLORIA: Yes, times are rather difficult. Money is tight. But surely a little chuck steak is in the budget for most? Perhaps a lamb chop or two?

BABS: Not much left over for luxuries these days is there? [*Pause.*] Things like meat. [*Pause.*] Or fresh air. [*Pause.*] Or sunlight on your face in the morning.

> *Pause.*

GLORIA: But there are benefits. Anyone who provides appropriate accommodation receives financial support.

BABS: Maybe it doesn't stretch to the meat budget. What with the extra Vegemite on the bill.

GLORIA: Still, we all should do our little bit, shouldn't we? It's the patriotic thing.

DONALD: All I know is, I can have up to half a side of beef left on any given day.

BABS: That's three and a half bullocks a week!

GLORIA: What are you saying, Donald?

DONALD: Truth be told, I came here for another reason ladies. It's not just a social call.

GLORIA: But I thought… the sausages…

DONALD: I need to ask a favour, Gloria.

GLORIA: Surely you're not suggesting—

DONALD: Gloria, I'm a butcher not a bureaucrat. The fact of the matter is, you have starving people living under your stairs and I have leftover food!

GLORIA: But what you're proposing is illegal!

BABS: It's against government policy.

GLORIA: It's bleeding heart bull.

BABS: It's… it's… it's… very kind.

GLORIA: I refuse to allow Peoples From Elsewhere Who Do Not Recognise Perfectly Good Borders to benefit illegally from my Land of Plenty! [*Pause.*] There are limits Donald! [*Pause.*] Look, I never thought I'd be the type to lock people up in a cupboard. [*Pause.*] In a cupboard under my stairs. [*Pause.*] I don't even like stairs. Never did. [*Pause.*] I have a bung hip, you see. [*Pause.*] Makes it difficult, to say the least. [*Pause.*] And as for locking people up, well… [*Pause.*] I think you've forgotten something. [*Pause.*] Something very important. [*Pause.*] It's a very big cupboard.

BABS: [*helpfully*] At least four feet wide.

GLORIA: I didn't realise you felt so strongly about the issue, Donald. [*Pause.*] Is this going to affect our courtship?

> SYLVIA *trots in and sits in the middle of the room, in full view of all three. She scratches lazily. She has a cardboard sign around her neck with a drawing of a window on it. They all stare at her. Silence.*

Cup of tea anyone?

> *Pause. They ignore* GLORIA *and continue to stare at* SYLVIA. *A long pause.*

DONALD: What an extraordinary thing.

BABS: Sylvia!

GLORIA: This must stop.

BABS: Perhaps it's just starting…

GLORIA: What concerns me most is: how did she get access to a pen and paper?

DONALD: Where there is a will, there is a way…

> *All three look at* SYLVIA. *Pause.* SYLVIA *passes wind. Slowly.*

GLORIA: Sylvia! You naughty girl! Take that offensive creature away Barbara!

BABS: Yes lovey. Shall I put the kettle on then? Tea anyone?

DONALD: I'd love a cuppa.

GLORIA: White with *one,* dear.

BABS: Back in a jiffy then. Come on, Sylvia.

> BABS *rises from the plastic covered couch and walks across the plastic carpet runner to the kitchen.* SYLVIA *pads after her.*

GLORIA: I must apologise Donald—I really don't know how much more of this I can take. Perhaps you could do something… after all—you're a butcher…

DONALD: Is that necessary Gloria? Sylvia's no bother to me. By the by, that's an interesting choice of name for a canine. Very distinguished.

GLORIA: Babs named her. After a poet or some such maudlin personage. She reads far too much…

DONALD: The dog does appear to have an artistic bent…

GLORIA: Indeed. Now, where were we? Ah yes, the sausages…

> GLORIA *giggles.*

> *Cross fade to* BABS *and* SYLVIA *in the kitchen.* BABS *fills the kettle and assembles the tea cups.*

BABS: Fancy that! Of all things! Did you hear all that Sylvia?

SYLVIA: I did. One sugar—fancy it. She's coming on a bit strong.

BABS: I didn't mean that exactly.

SYLVIA: I suppose he did bring her sausages…

BABS: I was talking about Donald's suggestion. About the meat.

SYLVIA: Of course.

BABS: Do you think he has a point?

SYLVIA: Well it's very contentious issue Babs, but like the man said, he does have leftovers.

BABS: It's certainly very *humane* of him. [*Pause.*] Sylvia—goodness, gracious—you're talking!

SYLVIA: Yes.

BABS: But—I—you—you've never spoken before!

SYLVIA: As they say, desperate times call for desperate measures. Maybe you just weren't listening hard enough. [*Pause.*] I mean, come on, Babs, what do I have to do? All the barking, the begging, the passing of wind—do you think that was all for my own amusement? Do you consider that normal behaviour?

BABS: Yes, well I do, rather. For a *dog*. [*Pause.*] Does Gloria know about this?

SYLVIA: I tried to strike up a conversation with her, but it turns out we don't see eye to eye...

BABS: I see. Sylvia, you don't think that Mrs Feathersworth let those peoples out *deliberately*, do you? [*Pause.*] But how could she do it? Go against government policy like that? We all have to do our bit, even if it means putting ourselves out. If it's for the greater good...

SYLVIA: Some sacrifice is to be expected, I suppose...

BABS: What will happen to the escapees, do you think?

SLYVIA: It won't be easy for them on the outside, that's a fact. But they've travelled too far to be locked in a sewing room. [*Pause.*] Or a cupboard under somebody's stairs.

BABS: I do have to admit Sylvia, it's dreadfully inconvenient. What with all their crying, the endless sandwich making and so on. It gets me quite anxious sometimes. Frankly I don't blame that Feathersworth woman!

SYLVIA: Why, those peoples under your stairs don't know how good they've got it! Free accommodation, all the Vegemite sangers they can eat...

BABS: Don't forget the jam ones for the children.

SYLVIA: The children, especially, are having a wonderful time. I heard them playing a game the other day. Something to do with aliens...

BABS: That doesn't sound nice.

SYLVIA: The baby's grown too. He's almost walking now...

BABS: I didn't know there was a baby! Of course, the little slipper!

SYLVIA: A child was born right there in the cupboard. You didn't hear the mother labouring?

BABS: I thought the screaming might have been part of some ritual—a cultural thing perhaps...

SYLVIA: Spoke his first word the other day. Do you know what it was?

BABS: No I'm afraid I don't...

SYLVIA: Me neither. I don't speak the language.

BABS: I do feel a tiny bit awful about them being stuck in that little cupboard without fresh air, natural light, or *immediate* access to running water...

SYLVIA: I'm sure they could catch the condensation from the roof...

BABS: After all Sylvia, it's probably a good thing that it's so dark in there. Then they can't see what they're missing out on. Us being the lucky country and all...

The kettle begins to boil/scream. It underscores the following section.

SYLVIA: Close your eyes, Babs.

BABS: Okay dear. What for?

SYLVIA: Don't you worry. Are they shut tight?

BABS: Yes dear.

SYLVIA: What do you see?

BABS: Nothing, of course.

SYLVIA: Press your hand to your eyes. Close out the light. Now what do you see?

BABS: Nothing dear. Only black.

SYLVIA: Press harder. Concentrate.

BABS: I am concentrating.

SYLVIA: Forget about everything else. Forget about trying to see something. Forget about remembering what was there before the darkness. What do you see?

BABS: I told you. Nothing dear. Blackness.

SYLVIA: Listen closely. Look past the black. Forget what you have been told, or what you know to be true. Look beyond your hands. Look beyond the colour of the dark. What do you see?

BABS: I... nothing really... maybe a hint of red? At the edges.

SYLVIA: Aha!

BABS: It's just a hint, mind... very faint.

SYLVIA: Don't open your eyes! Keep looking into the dark. What else do you see?

BABS: Maybe yellow. Yes, there's a stream of yellow in the centre of the darkness.

SYLVIA: Yes! Yes! And what else?

BABS: Near the red there's... purple. And pink! The pink is bordering the purple!

SYLVIA: Good, Good! Anything else?

BABS: There's orange too. And a bit of green beside the yellow? And blue. Sylvia, there's blue!

SYLVIA: So there is.

The kettle sings.

BABS: My goodness, it's a rainbow! A rainbow in the dark!

SYLVIA: That's why these people have come here, Babs. This is why they wait in the dark. Even under your stairs. This is why they have not Recognised Perfectly Good Borders. It is because they see colour beyond the darkness. They can see a rainbow in the dark.

The kettle switches off. Pause.

It's teatime, don't you think?

BABS *picks up the tea tray. They walk down the plastic carpet runner to the living room and* BABS *settles herself on the couch.* SYLVIA *snuffles at her feet.*

GLORIA: What on earth were you yelling about in the kitchen?

BABS: I was just chatting with Sylvia.

GLORIA: Really? And what did she have to say?

BABS: She was very vocal on one point actually—

DONALD: Gracious. Is that so?

GLORIA: Barbara, how absurd!

DONALD: Well now, Gloria, she *is* handy with a pen and paper, so I suppose it's not too much of a stretch…

There is a loud cry from under the stairs.

GLORIA: Babs dear, are you forgetting something?

BABS: Yes, of course. I'll attend to them, shall I?

GLORIA: Yes pet. Don't forget the sandwiches. And mind your nightgown this time. Don't let them grab you again. A torn slip is not very ladylike is it?

SYLVIA: Neither is a peach negligee if you ask me. Even if it *is* lined…

BABS: No dear, I won't. Come on, Sylvia.

BABS *rises from the plastic-covered couch. She walks down the plastic carpet runner to the cupboard under the stairs.* SYLVIA *trots after her.*

GLORIA: I tell you, it's not proper, Donald. It took me an age to stitch it up last time…

Fade to black.

The sound of BABS *and* SYLVIA's *footstep down the stairs. The sound of muffled cries increase as they approach the heavy cupboard door.* BABS *opens the door slowly. The sound of 'fear' rushes out. Silence.* BABS *sets down the plate of sandwiches. Pause.*

Half-light. BABS *and* SYLVIA *outside the cupboard door.*

BABS: [*whispering*] You, know, Sylvia, I've decided to open the window in here… to let the light in a bit.

SYLVIA: What a good idea, Babs. And while Gloria is otherwise entertained, I'll lead the way to the fresh air, shall I?

The sound of the window being opened and the prisoners climbing slowly out of the cupboard in small groups, talking softly amongst themselves in their own language. It underscores the following scene. Fade to black. Lights up on living room.

GLORIA: And as I was saying, Donald, it's all in the thread count. [*Pause.*] What is that noise, do you suppose?

DONALD: What noise? I beg your pardon?

GLORIA: That thumping—it sounds like—

DONALD: Let me just turn up my hearing aid dear—

GLORIA: But Donald you don't have a hearing aid!

DONALD: Why, that's very true dear—you're quite right—

GLORIA: It sounds like—Barbara! Where is she? She should be back by now.

DONALD: I don't mind her taking a little longer. If you know what I mean.

GLORIA: Oh, Donald!

DONALD: Gloria.

GLORIA: Oh, Donald…

DONALD: *Oh,* Gloria.

He kisses her. Suddenly the lights begin to flicker and change colour: red, orange, yellow, green, blue purple and pink. The room is bathed in all the colours of the rainbow.

GLORIA: Donald—it's the Peoples From Elsewhere Who Don't Recognise Perfectly Good Borders!

DONALD: Gloria!

He kisses her again.

GLORIA: Excuse me, Donald, how lovely, but I must check on Barbara!

She gets up to leave. He joins her.

DONALD: But Gloria, you don't even like stairs! And what about your bung hip?!

GLORIA: Some sacrifice is to be expected I suppose…

Fade to black. The sound of DONALD *and* GLORIA*'s laboured footsteps on the stairs. They push open the door to the cupboard. The room is bathed in light from the large open window.* BABS *is by the window looking out. The empty sandwich tray is on the floor.* GLORIA *and* DONALD *go over to her and look out.*

GLORIA: The Peoples From Elsewhere Who Don't Recognise Perfectly Good Borders!

DONALD: I can see them! Across the park. They are shining.

GLORIA: Do you think it was the sandwiches?

BABS: Well Vegemite *is* an acquired taste…

GLORIA: Maybe it was the accommodation, I will concede it was a touch cramped.

BABS: Yes there was distinct lack of elbowroom.

DONALD: Well there's so many of them! One, two, three… twenty-four, twenty-five!

BABS: Twenty-six, actually. At least six kids.

GLORIA: And a baby too.

BABS: Yes, he was born right there in the cupboard.

GLORIA: I made him slippers.

GLORIA *retrieves the slipper from her pocket.*

BABS: But you didn't say.

GLORIA: It wasn't in the handbook, dear.

BABS: Lots of things aren't pet.

GLORIA: It's just an example of the fact that life will prevail.

BABS: Simply a case in point that the spirit can't fail.

GLORIA: You know, I never noticed how nice the light in here could be.

BABS: Yes it looks much better now.

DONALD: Will they be alright, do you think? After all, they don't know the territory…

GLORIA: I hope you at least packed them a lunch Babs.

BABS: Yes, and filled them a thermos, dear. And look, they've got a guide.

DONALD: [*looking out the window*] It appears they are being led away by a small animal... is that a *dog*?

BABS: Of course. It's Sylvia.

GLORIA: We must give her a bone...

BABS: After all, it was all dreadfully inconvenient...

   Fade to black.

***

EPILOGUE

In darkness. A cupboard door closing. The sound of silence.

THE END

The PACIFIC Solution

A PLAY IN ONE ACT

BEN ELTHAM

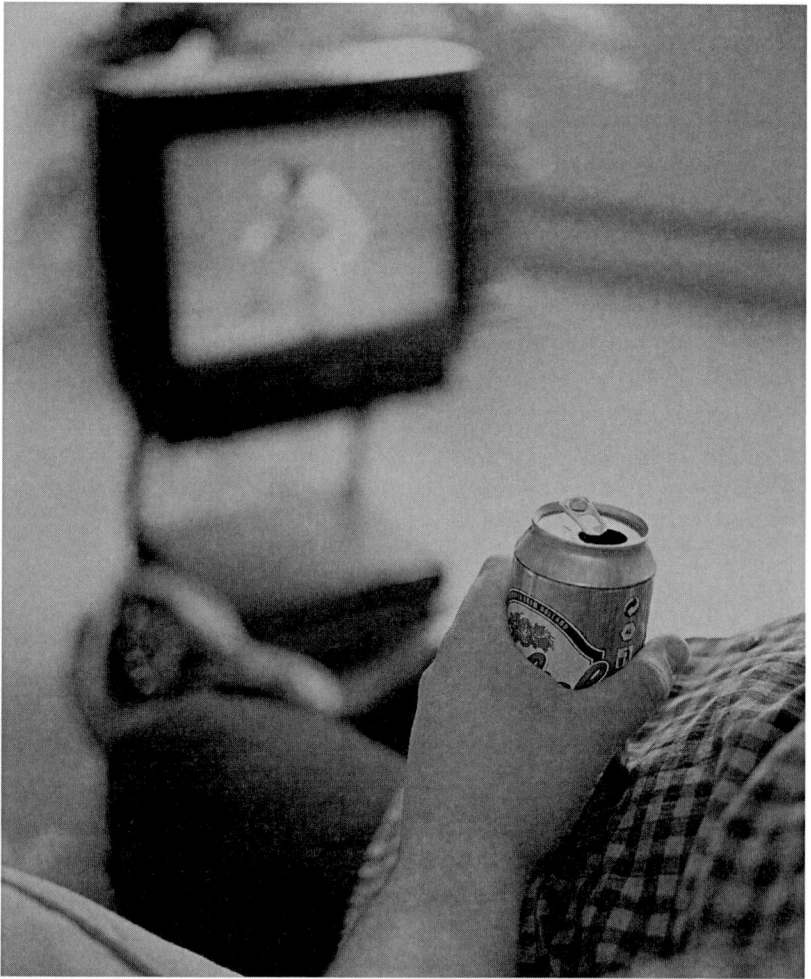

The Pacific Solution*'s Johnny: cricket, beer and the dark side of Australian mateship.*

Introduction

It is tantalising to speculate about what Ben Eltham's protagonist in *The Pacific Solution*, diehard cricket tragic and unabashed racist, Johnny, would make of Pakistan-born Usman Khawaja, the first Muslim to play for Australia. Or of Fawad Ahmed, a first class cricketer who fled northwest Pakistan in 2010 and whose application for Australian citizenship was fast-tracked following a legislative amendment in July 2013, making him eligible to play in this year's Ashes test series. Johnny represents a form of bullish Australian masculinity that has not traditionally made much space for difference. In their book chapter on 'hegemonic masculinity' and Australian sport, Jim McKay, Geoffrey Lawrence, Toby Miller and David Rowe observe that 'sport in Australia (as in most other countries) has a profoundly masculine inflection, operating as a major means through which ascendant forms of masculinity are asserted, promoted, tested and defended against "rival" articulations of masculinity and femininity' (p. 233). Johnny's love of the game is something his housemates, pothead Mandy and studious Phil, half-heartedly go along with, and while neither is scared of Johnny, his dominant, demanding personality nevertheless sucks them into his orbit.

The names of Eltham's characters were immediately resonant for Brisbane audiences at Metro Arts Theatre's 2006 production of *The Pacific Solution*: under Prime Minister John Howard, two successive Ministers for Immigration, Philip Ruddock and Amanda Vanstone, spearheaded indefinite and offshore detention and deterrence in Australia. During their years in public office, all three politicians clung with white-knuckled fervour to a party line that positioned asylum seekers as presumptuous queue jumpers who, in Ruddock's words, offended the 'sensitivities of Australians' with their 'practice unknown in our culture' of sewing lips shut during prolonged extrajudicial incarceration.

In the play, Johnny has committed himself to seeing every ball of the 2005 Ashes series and keeps up a stream of commentary which housemate Mandy half listens to as she tends their 'Orchy-bottle bong'. Johnny's armchair expertise is funny; it's also impassioned and erudite in the same way ABC TV's weekly sports discussion show *Offsiders* is, and will be happily familiar to *The Pacific Solution*'s cricket-literate readers, to the extent that some may find themselves mentally agreeing, countering, adding or detracting. The conversation's shift, then, to Johnny's (and to a slightly lesser degree, Mandy's) rage over 'dole bludgers', 'lefties', 'Abos', 'Goths', 'Pakis' and taxation, prompts readers to adjust their responses to these chilled-out Aussies. When law student Phil enters, we get a taste of a more cerebral set of prejudices that contrast with Johnny and Mandy's knee-jerk ones.

Halfway through the play, the housemates are interrupted by the arrival at their front door of an Iraqi asylum seeker, Asif, who requests their protection. Instead, Asif is knocked unconscious by Johnny and forced into a cupboard. Level-headed Phil—who, Eltham notes with irony, is 'President of the local University's chapter of Amnesty International'—devises a means of dealing with Asif and of absolving the housemates of responsibility for him. Phil's eureka moment, gleaned from his study of the *Residential Tenancies Act*, is a piece of pure bureaucratic sophistry:

> PHIL: The Act states that we have no responsibility to look after him if he's not on our property. Therefore I propose that we excise the cupboard from the lease, for the purposes of being able to refuse responsibility for [*to* JOHNNY] not only for the thrashing he appears already to have received, but for his physical well-being *prior, during* and *following* his 'request', which is now, legally, rendered null and void, in that there is no legal basis for it to have happened at all.

This is, of course, a satire on Australia's notorious excision legislation—a cornerstone of the 'Solution' from which the play takes its name—first implemented in 2001 with the removal of certain maritime territories from Australia's migration zone and since extended, as I shall explain. While it doesn't affect Australia's vast Exclusive Economic Zone (which protects the nation's rights over exploration and marine resources) *or* the rights of Australian citizens and visa holders to travel within and across excised places, excision means that asylum seekers intercepted in an *excised offshore place* never legally 'arrive' in Australia at all in the sense that they are excluded from applying directly for Australian protection visas.

At first glance, the premise of *The Pacific Solution* bears striking similarities to that of Victoria Carless's *The Rainbow Dark*, but the plays' respective use of the domestic space as an analogy for immigration detention and the impulses underpinning it differ in crucial ways. Carless's characters ultimately decide that another form of community is possible. Eltham's satire has a darker edge. Johnny, Phil and Mandy aren't just feckless losers, but a vicious trio whose response to Asif seems ultimately to suggest that a drive to exclude may represent the underbelly of Australian mateship. When they find themselves backed into a corner (partly of their own making), they turn to blunt bureaucracy. In the end, the letter of the law, not Asif's call for help, 'human being to human being', is the means by which they will acknowledge the stranger in their midst.

The passage of time since the play was written has overlaid Eltham's picture of suburban ennui in ways few would have predicted. Today, Johnny would have to deal with the double blow of figuring out how Khawaja and Ahmed fit into his worldview *and* contemplating the waning of Australia's once formidable dominance of international test cricket. But Phil would likely cheer Johnny with the prospect of even greater scope to disavow Asif. Under a legislative amendment passed in May 2013, territorial excision now encompasses the entire continent of Australia. Transposing this to the world of *The Pacific Solution*, the 'logical' response of Johnny, Phil and Mandy to Asif's arrival would be to excise their entire sharehouse from its own lease agreement. In this way, there would be no circumstance in which Asif could arrive uninvited and unannounced at the house and expect to be let in.

Emma Cox

The Pacific Solution was first produced by Metro Arts Theatre, as part of the Brisbane Festival, at the Metro Arts Theatre, Brisbane, on 25 July 2006, with the following cast and crew:

JOHNNY	Jonathan Brand
MANDY	Louise Brehmer
PHIL	Lucas Stibbard
ASIF	Amin Deering

Director, Marcel Dorney

DIRECTOR'S NOTE

As Emma Cox writes in her introduction, Ben's satire of Anglo-Australian attitudes towards refugees opens firmly within the prevalent frame of suburban Australian realism, complete with sport, masculinity, and free-flowing beer. By the time Asif turned up, the audience of the original production—largely composed of the student-into-professional class from which these characters were sketched—had been made comfortable, by Jonathan, Louise and Lucas' pitch-perfect portrayals, and by the specificity of Ben's writing. To turn the identification of the audience around is hardly a new trick, but it's executed here with skill, and —in a way that sets it apart from much Australian 'political theatre'—for a well thought-out polemical purpose. It's surprisingly uncommon for a first-time playwright to draw an audience in so firmly and retain his nerve to deliver the punch, but it was, after all, Ben's trenchant political intellect that persuaded me to work on this with him in the first place. It's intriguing to think—from a position seven years later—about the way those members of the audience unfamiliar with the specifics of Australia's refugee policy laughed at the sheer absurdity of Amanda's final plan. You could tell the ones who read the newspaper; they laughed, too, but the laughter was a very different colour.

Marcel Dorney, June 2013

CHARACTERS

JOHNNY, a young man, short and balding but powerful, with big eyebrows and glasses, who runs a petrol station in suburban Australia.

MANDY, a slightly overweight, frumpy young woman who works on the front desk of the local Centrelink. She speaks with a suburban accent and likes wearing shirts with loud prints and riotous colours.

PHIL, a tall, thin, pale, serious young man who is studying law. He is from a rich suburb and is President of the local University's chapter of Amnesty International.

ASIF, an Iraqi refugee.

DESIGN AND SETTING

The living room of a typical Australian share-house in June 2005.

There are three large, shabby couches which surround a long, crowded, messy coffee table. On the coffee table is an Orchy-bottle bong, a chop bowl, scissors, a large bag of hydroponic marijuana, several remote controls, coffee mugs and glasses, ashtrays, men's magazines and sports sections of newspapers. There is a television—always on—which the characters stare towards, and which the audience can't see, but which sound effects tell us is tuned constantly to Fox Sports 1.

Along the back wall, left, is the front door of the share-house. Stage left represents the corridor to the kitchen, toilet and bedrooms of this 3-bedroom brick bungalow house. There is also a door to a small closet or cupboard, near the front door to the house.

On the couch, centre, sits JOHNNY holding the remote control and drinking a stubby of Carlton Draught beer. He is watching Fox Sports 1. Beside him, on the right couch, sits MANDY, methodically chopping marijuana into the bowl.

There is a soundtrack to certain moments of this play, and that soundtrack is a thirty-second loop of television cricket commentary from a boring part of a day's play. (This loop can be recorded and manufactured easily by anyone who has access to cricket on radio or television.) The lights should stay up and this commentary loop should play for about forty-five seconds in the breaks between scenes.

A note about lighting: there should be no follow-spots or special stage lighting in the play. Any lights that are used should represent normal 60W or 80W household globes, and they should stay up all the time.

SCENE ONE

TELEVISION COMMENTARY: Coming up later tonight… The Ashes! See every ball live on Fox Sports 1.

JOHNNY: Woo-hoo! You bewdy!

MANDY: You bloody ripper.

JOHNNY: Bloody unreal. [*Pause.*] I'm so excited.

MANDY: Are you going to stay up all night watching cricket again, Johnny?

JOHNNY: Mate. Ashes. Cricket. See—every—ball.

MANDY: Fuck. You're going to be tired tomorrow.

JOHNNY: Beer—cones—cricket. Beer—cones—*cricket*. Ashes cricket. Bretty Lee throwing 'em down at 90 miles per hour Mandy, Lords, the home of cricket, look it's got everything absolutely everything and I wish I was there.

MANDY: What time's your shift tomorrow? Isn't it 6 o'clock?

JOHNNY: C'mon Mandy, grow some fucking balls.

Pause. MANDY *doesn't answer; she's busy chopping marijuana.*

It's the First Test in living memory that might actually be bloody interesting. Harmison mate. Freddy Flintoff. Simon Jones with the reverse swing later in the innings. Even Hoggard's a bit under-rated actually, actually if I can say that, I think Hoggard's really quite a penetrating bowler early on. It's one of the finest fast bowling quartets assembled against Australia since the great West Indian pace attacks of the '80s and early '90s. [*Pause.*] I'm sure you remember Ambrose and Walsh at their peak, they were really something pretty special and I have to say this Australian team is not travelling that well, they really aren't, they're looking vulnerable and it's going to make for some wonderful cricket, surely one of the closest series in years. [*Pause.*] I think the Poms could do it. [*Pause.*] Flintoff's good, hey.

MANDY: Yeah, but we've got Warney.

JOHNNY: Warney's a trooper, don't worry about that. He'll tie one end down. And then with McGrath at the other end—

MANDY: Warney's a fat, balding womaniser. He's doing most of his damage with his mobile phone.

JOHNNY: [*getting agitated*] Now don't you start on about Warney, Amanda. Warney's a great. He is a great. He is a true Australian legend. When you are talking about leg-spin bowling in test history, there is no-one who can claim to come close to Warnie's achievements, although of course it's risky to compare eras and Bradman did maintain that Tiger O'Reilly was the bowler he least liked to face—

MANDY: I'd say plenty of English nurses would say Warney's the bowler they'd least like to face—

JOHNNY: Close to 600 wickets Amanda. The man has taken close to 600 wickets. He's an Australian legend and he'd be the second picked in my team of the century, I can tell you that right now, along with Keith Miller, McGrath, Steve Waugh, Victor Trumper, Greg Chappell, Sid Barnes to open, obviously a 1972-era Lillee would be a walk-up start to take the new ball—

MANDY: Funnily enough Johnny, you've actually told me before who's in your Australian Cricket Team of the Century—

JOHNNY: Third pace bowler is always tricky. I lean towards Lindwall as a left-armer and a great partner to Miller. You see with Miller in the team you could play a second spinner. There's your bowling allrounder right there in Keith Miller.

MANDY: What about Merv? Merv had the best moustache in Australian cricket history.

JOHNNY: You only say that—[*Pause.*] You only say that—because he's all you've seen with a decent moustache. *Actually* if you look at some of the photos of early Australian cricket teams you'll see some *champion* moustaches of the *most florid variety*.

MANDY: And Mardo. He's pretty cute.

JOHNNY: It's not about good looks. Australian cricketers have never been good looking. We've *never* been good looking. We're a bunch of ugly sledging cunts and that's why we win, Mandy.

MANDY: I've heard some disgusting things about Steve Waugh from Sharon when she worked at Club CBD. Said they all had *terrible* language problems. And dirty. No wonder their marriages all break up.

JOHNNY: Their marriages do not all break up Mandy. Steve Waugh's marriage has not broken up. Some player's marriages broke down but you've got to expect that with all the touring, and just the amount of one-day cricket they play these days, it's very hard on the players—

MANDY: And the texting, and the dirty drinking binges with Kevin Pietersen.

JOHNNY: Now see, Pietersen is good. He's got the X-factor. I think he's going to do something special. Warney'll get him though. Warney's definitely my spinner in the Team of the Century, although I think you could possibly play Benaud or Grimmett if it was a turning wicket.

MANDY: Is Gilly in there?

JOHNNY: I think it's a very interesting decision about wicket-keeping, I think most people say Healy was a better gloveman—and of course Marsh—but I think the excitement that Gilchrist brings to the lower order and just the way he's changed the game…

MANDY: [*still methodically chopping*] Healy's funnier, though, when he commentates. I think Gilly's got big ears. *And that ad!* For Castrol car oil.

JOHNNY: [*agitated*] That's a good ad, Mandy, it's a bloody good ad.

MANDY: Oh come on John. You think every ad featuring an Australian cricketer is a good ad. You even liked that McDonalds ad where David Boon eats the Big Mac.

JOHNNY: [*sighing reverentially*] Booney.

MANDY: Steve Waugh. See he's a dirty bastard according to Sharon.

JOHNNY: Yeah Steve Waugh at number 5. Miller at 6, Gilchrist at 7. Or you could even open with Gilly. [*Pause.*] It is a funny ad that one. [*Adopting an unconvincing Indian accent*] 'Not long now, Mr Gilly'. [*He laughs.*] I like that one, it's funny.

MANDY: You are fucking stupid sometimes.

JOHNNY: Chill out, Amanda.

MANDY: No, you're a fucking idiot. The way you believe in these ads.

JOHNNY: Now if I may say, Amanda—

MANDY: Do you like the beer ads too, Johnny?

JOHNNY: I like some beer ads.

MANDY: Can you identity with… the Bundy Bear?

JOHNNY: What are you—

MANDY: Are you the sort of guy who goes out and buys Carlton Draught because of their amusingly tongue-in-cheek 'Made from Beer' campaign?

JOHNNY: No.

MANDY: Look, you're drinking a Carlton Draught now.

JOHNNY: Now it's not like that, Mandy. I still drink VB at the pub. I actually mainly drink premium beers these days as you well know. I just bought a six-pack of Carlton Draught home the other day because it was on special; in fact it was cheaper than VB. It's not a bad drop. They drink it in Melbourne a lot.

MANDY: It's VB with a red label you goose.

JOHNNY: No it's not.

MANDY: Completely identical.

JOHNNY: How do you know?

MANDY: Mate of mine—

JOHNNY: No, hang on. *How* could you *possibly* know?

MANDY: [*speaking slowly and sarcastically*] A—mate—of mine—from Melbourne—told me. Mate of Phil's too actually, you remember Wazza?

JOHNNY: Wazza?

MANDY: Yeah, you know Wazza, he had that poofy moustache until Phil told him he looked like the guy from *Boogie Nights* and so he shaved it? Yeah, well, anyway, *Wazza* used to work at CUB in Melbourne and he reckons that it's completely identical. They brew it all up and then stick a new red label on it to keep the marketing guys happy. It's all marketing Johnny, and you've fallen for it.

JOHNNY: Well I reckon VB's got a slightly fishy taste that Carlton Draught doesn't have.

MANDY: Yeah well Wazza reckons *that's* from straining it through fish scales. You want a cone?

JOHNNY: Yeah, alright.

> MANDY *packs a cone and hands* JOHNNY *the bong. He takes a lighter from his pocket and smokes it in one long toke, exhaling the smoke upwards with practiced glee. The TV continues to blather on in the background while they sit silently.*

I think you've got to play Warnie, he does so much for team morale.

MANDY: You got the lighter? It's my turn.
JOHNNY: Oh, sorry.

MANDY smokes the cone.

Lights stay up and there's forty-five seconds of mindless cricket commentary to end the scene.

SCENE TWO

JOHNNY: So how was work today?
MANDY Oh you know, the usual.

MANDY busies herself with the bong—cleaning it, removing and stoking the cone piece, investigating the seal on the hose.

JOHNNY: The usual?
MANDY: Yeah, you know.
JOHNNY: No I don't know, Mandy. I do not know what the usual is. Believe it or not I do not go to Centrelink every day, and although it's true I have once been inside a Centrelink to get the rent off you when you forgot it last month, my lone visit was not enough for me to know what the usual is.
MANDY: Well, you know… It's mainly students enrolling and trying to get Youth Allowance, students quitting and trying to get Newstart, long-term dole bludgers trying to dodge out of their mutual obligation—the usual.
JOHNNY: Fucking dole bludgers, they make my blood boil.
MANDY: You should try processing fortnightly forms.
JOHNNY: I mean, it's just the way they act about it…
MANDY: Hmmm.
JOHNNY: Just the way they think it's their right to get the dole. I mean some of these characters have never worked a real day in their life.
MANDY: Hmmm.
JOHNNY: It's like the world owes them a living, Mandy!
MANDY: I know.
JOHNNY: It's those lefties I really hate. The hippies getting paid by people like you to spend their lives organising protests. Doing

arts degrees so they can learn all about *feminism*, and *saving the refugees*. It's our taxes that pays for that, Mandy!

MANDY: Just settle down. Our taxes pay for my job Johnny.

JOHNNY: Too bloody right! Do you know how much grief I cop when the petrol price goes up? People blame me! They don't even realise the government takes 40 per cent.

JOHNNY: It's a tax on a tax Mandy! There's petrol excise, there's GST on fuel, and then there's GST on excise! It's outrageous.

MANDY: I know.

JOHNNY: Don't you bloody 'I know' me, it's a serious issue facing my industry.

> MANDY *is silent as she continues to give the bong a solid spring clean.*

Like the bloody boongs.

MANDY: I'm sorry?

JOHNNY: Oh those bloody Abos. You know exactly what I'm talking about; surely I don't have to use the politically correct term in my own house.

MANDY: Well I don't work the Abstudy line you know, they've got me on the students and dole bludgers mate.

JOHNNY: There's white people who just go out and *give* these people money, Mandy, as though that's going to solve their bloody petrol-sniffing! There's an Aboriginal Industry, Mandy, I was listening to Alan Jones go on about it just the other day.

MANDY: Yes, well we're not lucky enough to get Mr Jones in at Chateau Centrelink. We have to make do with Triple M.

JOHNNY: Did you know—did you realise Mandy—there are actually whole firms of lawyers who specialise in native title law? Whole bloody law firms of them. It's Ally McBeal for the bloody Aboriginals, and I'm sick of it!

MANDY: Hmmm.

JOHNNY: Well you should know, you must get whole tribes of 'em coming into Centrelink every day.

MANDY: What I hate is the Goths. The skanky Goths with bad make-up and drug addictions. Oooh-hoo-hoo. [*She shudders*]. I just can't stand those Goths, they give me the willies. How can they go out with *that make-up on*?

JOHNNY: Well I know one thing. We shouldn't be paying dole to Gothics. [*He addresses the audience*] I think that's something everyone here can agree on.

MANDY: Definitely.

JOHNNY: I mean I can even cop the odd poofter or two, you know. I don't mind the old gay lord, as long as they don't… you know… as long as they stay on the other side of the counter. And anyway, most of 'em have got great jobs. Graphic designers and advertising executives mate. They make out like bandits.

MANDY: Fashion designers.

JOHNNY: Too bloody right. Hairdressers are the new plumbers, they're making $70, $80 an hour these days. It's unbelievable.

MANDY: I'm pretty sure my hairdresser is straight, actually.

JOHNNY: No kids either. You know, fewer expenses to worry about. Condoms. Pinot noir. Bit of Ikea furniture. I guess there's the expensive haircuts and facials and all that. Even so, no need to spend their money on beer or the horses or a season ticket to the footy or anything. None of your typical bloke expenses. I tell you, it's a lot cheaper being a gay man.

MANDY: How could you *possibly* know John?

JOHNNY: But the bloody university students… I mean, why do we give them any money at all?

MANDY: Well we don't really, youth allowance and AUSTUDY is less than the dole even.

JOHNNY: Well they should be *paying their own way* Mandy. Get a part-time job, for God's sake. It's not too hard to get a job in this country, if you really want to work. You should send some of these dole bludgers down to the servo Mandy, I'll give 'em a job on the graveyard shift straight away.

MANDY: Yes, but you sacked the last guy I sent to you, John, remember?

JOHNNY: No, that's not true. I cut back on Ravi's shifts, didn't I? Well, he was useless, wasn't he?

MANDY: I don't—

JOHNNY: Well you do know, I told you. Repeatedly.

MANDY: Yes, I still think you should have given him a chance.

JOHNNY: Admit it yourself. Was he useless? Yes he was.

MANDY: He wasn't that useless. He had a lovely smile.

JOHNNY: And was he useless, Mandy?

MANDY: I don't know John—

JOHNNY: And was he useless?

MANDY: [*speaking loudly now to get her point across*]. *I don't know John*—I wasn't there. Like—der!

JOHNNY: Well he was bloody useless, Mandy, he couldn't reconcile his till. I thought those Pakis were meant to be good with money. This guy could barely count.

MANDY: He had a computer science degree—

JOHNNY: Yeah well maybe he should have stuck to that, because he couldn't reconcile a till to save his life. I mean, you give a bloke a chance, and they let you down. They just let you down.

MANDY: But didn't Ravi like cricket?

JOHNNY: I'm not saying he wasn't a lovely bloke. He was. I liked the fellow. But he fell asleep at the counter. Some bloke drove up to the pump and put a full tank in, drove away without Ravi even noticing. We only worked it out when his pumps didn't add with the till and I had to go back through the security tapes.

MANDY: [*sighing*] That was a real shame.

JOHNNY: Well, we took it out of his pay cheque before we sacked him. You've got to make your till add up. I can't be held responsible if you go to sleep with the pumps left on. We're not running a charity… though we were for a while when employing your Sri Lankan friend.

Pause. Cricket commentary. JOHNNY *is suddenly engrossed again in the cricket.*

MANDY: Another cone?

JOHNNY: Yeah all right. It's going to be quite an exciting session; it's probably worth another cone before the second session starts up.

MANDY *and then* JOHNNY *smoke a cone each.*

Lights stay up and there's forty-five seconds of mindless cricket commentary to end the scene.

SCENE THREE

PHIL *enters through the front door. He is carrying a neat-looking rucksack over the shoulder of his fashionable t-shirt and holding a sheath of lecture notes in his hand.*

PHIL: Well, what have we here? Smoking, ahem, controlled substances again?

JOHNNY: Hi Phil.

MANDY: Do you want a cone, Phil?

PHIL: No thank you, I'll remind you that smoking marijuana is illegal.

JOHNNY: Is that your chief objection to it, Phil?

PHIL: Yes.

MANDY: Really?

PHIL: There are still substantial criminal penalties for marijuana possession and sale, even in this era of judicial activism, revolving-door prison sentences and our Courts' disgusting tolerance of what remains a Schedule one drug.

JOHNNY: I love it when you talk dirty, Phil.

PHIL: I would also remind you all that there are significant health problems associated with the abuse of illegal drugs.

JOHNNY: No shit, Phil.

PHIL: Research shows that smoking three joints a day can lead to the equivalent lung damage of twelve cigarettes. That's half a pack a day. And I would add, further to that, that the marijuana smokers of *this* house worsen the damage by smoking it in a water pipe and cutting it with tobacco.

MANDY: The word is spin, Phil, we *spin* it with tobacco.

PHIL: Well that's precisely right Mandy, and I'd draw your attention to the fact that you are destroying your lungs and your short-term memory and massively elevating your risk of cancer, so no I don't want a cone, as you call it.

JOHNNY: Beers in the fridge Phil.

MANDY: Can you bring one for us as well?

JOHNNY: Yeah, thanks Phil.

PHIL *exits down the corridor to file his lecture notes in his room.*

MANDY: I think Phil's taking all these law lectures a bit too seriously.

JOHNNY: It's the health warnings you should take note of; you smoke too much, Mandy.

MANDY: Oh you can talk Johnny. How much exercise have we been getting lately?

JOHNNY: I went for a walk the other morning. And last weekend I played touch, in fact I was thinking the other day that Phil and I should go and have a hit of tennis.

MANDY: I didn't know you even had a racket.

JOHNNY: I certainly do, and it's a good one too, Wilson, titanium head, great racket-head speed, quality shock-absorption, for the all-court player who feels at home on all surfaces. [*He stands up and begins to mime practising his ground-strokes.*] Wimbledon's on soon, isn't it?

> PHIL *comes back in with three beers, two of which he distributes to* JOHNNY *and* MANDY.

Oh thanks Phil! [*Opening beer*] You're a trooper, cobber.

PHIL: Carlton Draft, John? I saw you laughing at that 'Made From Beer' ad last night.

JOHNNY: I wasn't laughing.

PHIL: Your mouth [*Pause*] was open, and there were, ahem, *chuckling sounds* emanating from it.

MANDY: Ah hah!

JOHNNY: All right, no more bullshit, Phil.

MANDY: You are so full of shit, John.

JOHNNY: I am… not.

> *Pause.*

MANDY: Well, cheers. [*Opening beer*] A true Aussie hero Phil, and I thank you for it.

> JOHNNY *and* MANDY *clink beers with* PHIL.

JOHNNY: Cheers.

MANDY: Up ya bum.

PHIL: No worries mate.

MANDY: How was the lecture, Phil?

PHIL: It wasn't too bad. I'd say it was a reasonably interesting lecture, yes.

MANDY: What do they actually teach you in law anyway?

PHIL: Today we studied torts, or the law of civil wrongs.

JOHNNY: How to chase ambulances hey, Phil? Stub any toes you needed to sue for lately? What if I told you that lawyers are nothing but a bunch of fucking parasites?

MANDY: That's a bit harsh, John.

> *Pause.*

PHIL: I'm… out-*raged* at your scurrilous suggestion John, and I'd like you to withdraw it.

JOHNNY: Oooohhh—

PHIL: I'd like you—

JOHNNY: He wants me to withdraw it now!

PHIL: To withdraw it, as it is untrue and quite outrageous. Any suggestion that I am acting in any way other than in the best interests of—this—household—is completely dishonest, and I may add quite unsubstantiated. I am studying law to try and help the people of this nation—

JOHNNY: Oooohhhhh!

PHIL: And I am in fact an office bearer of the campus Amnesty Association, an office I am both intensely proud of and duty-bound to defend against unwarranted—in fact scurrilous—outrageous—assaults, particularly against a noble profession whose job it is to help interpret and administer the golden thread of justice— [*He pauses, licks his lips.*] and the Rule Of Law which holds our democracy together.

> *Pause.*

MANDY: Great speech, Phil.

JOHNNY: Yeah, a cracker.

> *A long pause.* PHIL *waits quietly but tensely for his apology.*

All right, I withdraw my remarks. There you go.

PHIL: Thank you. Now, I'm going to my room to study.

JOHNNY: Knock yourself out, Phil-baby.

MANDY: Don't listen to him Phil, he's just doing it to get a rise out of you.

> PHIL *exits.*

I think you might have pissed Phil off then, Johnny.

JOHNNY: Oh come on, he needs a rev every now and then to keep him interested.

MANDY: You attacked his legal studies, you know he hates that.

JOHNNY: Bloody lawyers; too many of them in the world already.

MANDY: C'mon, you'd love to be a lawyer. You're just saying that because you work at a service station.

JOHNNY: Service station work is a noble job. It's keeping people on the road it is, Mandy, it's keeping our $800 billion economy on the road. Not to mention all the free lighters I bring home, which I don't notice you complaining about.

MANDY: Yeah all right, no need to arc up.

JOHNNY: No, I'm not, I'm just giving Phil a rev.

MANDY: Yeah well I reckon you should go a little easier.

JOHNNY: Oh look Phil doesn't mind. [*Yelling*] Hey Phil, you don't mind it when I give you a rev, do you mate?

No answer from PHIL.

[*Louder*] *Do you mate?*

MANDY: He's not going to answer Johnny, you've pissed him off too much.

JOHNNY *gets up and walks over to stage left, where he yells even more loudly into the wings.*

JOHNNY: Hey Phil, you don't mind it when I tease you about chasin' ambulances, do you mate?

PHIL: [*offstage*] Would you be quiet please, John? I'm trying to study.

JOHNNY: [*walking back to the couch and sitting down*] I think Phil needs to get out a bit more Mandy. All this study's making him tense.

MANDY: Yeah.

JOHNNY: See! I told you he didn't mind. [*Pause.*] Another beer?

MANDY: [*packs another cone*] Yeah, all right.

Lights stay up and there's forty-five seconds of mindless cricket commentary to end the scene.

SCENE FOUR

MANDY: [*chopping again*] What did you want to be in school, John?

JOHNNY: What did I want to be in school?

MANDY: Yeah.

JOHNNY: What did I want to be in school?

MANDY: Yes John, that's what I asked.

JOHNNY: I wanted to captain the cricket team. Pathetic really. They never choose spin bowlers to be captain.

MANDY: No, I mean, what did you want to be *after* you left school.

JOHNNY: After school?

MANDY: You know, when you grew up.

JOHNNY: Well, I never had tickets on myself. I never thought I could play Shield or anything, First Grade would have done me fine. But you know, you have these dreams, you give it your best shot, but ultimately there's only eleven places aren't there, and there's some talented kids running around in the lower grades these days.

MANDY: No, I mean outside of sport. What did you want to *be* when you grew up?

JOHNNY: Well I don't know Mandy. What did *you* want to be?

MANDY: I wanted to be a pharmacist.

JOHNNY: You? [*He explodes into laughter.*] *You* wanted to be a chemist?

MANDY: Yeah.

JOHNNY: A chemist. Like, Green Spot chemists? Selling tinea cream and glucose jellybeans?

MANDY: Yeah.

JOHNNY: I find that pretty amusing, Mandy.

MANDY: Why?

JOHNNY: Don't you think you might have had a bit of a problem with the stock?

MANDY: No… what do you mean?

> JOHNNY *makes a crude gesture holding one nostril closed and sniffing loudly.*

You're such a prick sometimes, John.

JOHNNY: Says Mandy as she packs another cone. [*He gets up and walks over to stage left.*] Hey, Phil! Mandy's offering you another cone.

PHIL: [*from offstage*] I'm trying to study, John.

MANDY: Just leave Phil alone, will you? He's trying to study. Your shit isn't funny, John.

JOHNNY: Oh, it's *not funny* anymore!

MANDY: That's right.

JOHNNY: What?

MANDY: You are a total cunt you know sometimes, John. Why do you insult your flatmates so much?

JOHNNY: Oh have a cry Mandy. Do you want some tissues?

MANDY: You just missed a wicket.

JOHNNY: [*singing*] Don't cry baby Mummy's here…

MANDY: Gilchrist gone…

JOHNNY [*running over to couch quickly to see the wicket*] Ooooh noooo!

MANDY: Isn't he meant to be in your Team of the Century?

JOHNNY: Shut up Mandy, this isn't a time for jokes. Australia's in deep trouble here.

> *Pause.*

MANDY: Who's that bloke? He's quite cute.

JOHNNY: Flintoff.

MANDY: He's quite handsome.

> JOHNNY *curses inaudibly.*

Is he England's best player then?

JOHNNY [*agitated*] Did you see the reverse swing he's getting? No wonder Gilly's struggling.

MANDY: Hmmm, I quite like him. You get quite a good view of their bums in those white trousers.

JOHNNY: Mandy! Please!

> *Pause.*

MANDY: So.

JOHNNY: Yes. [*Pause.*] Australia's in trouble.

MANDY: Six down is bad, isn't it?

JOHNNY: It's not good for this many runs.

MANDY: Australia might lose.

JOHNNY: There's plenty of cricket left in this match. Warney doesn't need much to bowl with. It's early in the series. [*Pause.*] We're playing like crap.

Long pause.

MANDY: No, but, I mean, sport aside, what were your dreams Johnny?

JOHNNY: Dreams are a waste of fucking time.

MANDY: That's a horrible thing to say.

JOHNNY: [*angrily*] Well where are your dreams Mandy? How close does your pharmacy seem as you stamp dole diaries all afternoon?

MANDY: [*quietly*] Fuck you, Johnny.

JOHNNY: Well, fuck you.

Long pause.

[*Stiffly*] I'm regretful if I caused any offence with that previous remark.

MANDY: Jesus—you can't even apologise properly.

JOHNNY: Yes I can.

MANDY: Well do it then.

JOHNNY: Well I will.

MANDY: When?

JOHNNY: Soon.

MANDY: When is that, exactly?

JOHNNY: Well, ahh, I will, um, er, apologise when I believe it is in the best interests, um, of this household, that I do so.

MANDY: What's fucking wrong with you? [*Pause.*] Where's your life going John? I haven't noticed any promotions for you lately?

JOHNNY: [*encouraged*] That's more like it. Get a bit angry Mandy. I was just giving you a rev.

MANDY: You mean: taking out your own career frustrations on me.

JOHNNY: I love working at the servo Mandy. It's great. I'm helping Australia's $800 billion economy—

MANDY: $800 billion economy—

JOHNNY: Stay on the road.

MANDY: Stay on the road.

JOHNNY: Well yes, Mandy, that's right, I am helping. I am indeed.

MANDY: And what about the greenhouse gases, John?

JOHNNY: What the fuck?

MANDY: The greenhouse effect. You know, global warming?

JOHNNY: Oh don't give me that crap Mandy, global warming's a myth.

MANDY: A myth?

JOHNNY: Yeah, it's a myth. Haven't you been listening to Jonesy? It's all been cooked up by the greenies Mandy. To try and scare us.

MANDY: You are so full of it sometimes, John.

JOHNNY: It all goes in cycles, Amanda, that's what I heard. The earth has been warming naturally ever since the bloody ice age.

MANDY: Alright. Fine. So you're honestly saying to me that you *want* to be a servo sales clerk.

JOHNNY: [*suddenly exploding, slamming his beer down on the coffee table*] Now you fucking listen to me. *Do not* question my lifestyle. Don't you fucking dare, or I will—

MANDY: What, Johnny?

JOHNNY: Don't you fucking question me Mandy or so help me I will teach you a lesson.

> *Pause.*

MANDY: Yes?

JOHNNY: A lesson you will never forget, Mandy, girl or no girl, *do not* fucking tempt me.

MANDY: Is that a threat is it, Johnny?

JOHNNY: [*getting up menacingly*] It is a promise, Mandy, a fucking promise.

MANDY: I mean, can you get promoted from servo attendant? You don't exactly have an Engineering degree do you, Johnny?

JOHNNY: For Chrissakes Mandy I warned you not to push me. [*Yelling*] Do not fucking question me Mandy, or I will fucking arc up like you have never seen before.

MANDY: Oh, really.

JOHNNY: Yes.

MANDY: Johnny, why don't have another beer. You're looking tense, mate.

JOHNNY: No I'm not. [*A beat.*] Do *you* want another beer?

MANDY: Sure.

JOHNNY: Well I'll go get one then.

MANDY: Uh huh.

JOHNNY: You don't even fucking like Carlton Draft.

MANDY: Feeling a bit thirsty, John.

> JOHNNY *gets up and walks towards kitchen door, then pauses.*

JOHNNY: *Do not* fucking manipulate me Mandy.

MANDY: Hey John. You'll feel better after another beer, John.

JOHNNY: Okay.

> JOHNNY *exits. Lights stay up and there's forty-five seconds of mindless cricket commentary to end the scene.*

SCENE FIVE

PHIL *enters.*

PHIL: Australia in trouble.

MANDY: Not looking good.

PHIL: Johnny's not going to like the score.

MANDY: [*laughing*] Johnny's going to be so cut! We're fucked.

PHIL: We could fight back Mandy.

MANDY: We're fucked. Australia's going to lose the Ashes, Phil.

PHIL: That remains to be seen. And while I'm in agreeance with you on the facts of the situation, I would only concur in so far as being amused at our housemate's annoyance.

MANDY: Yeah, but don't you think it's good for the game that Australia loses sometimes at cricket?

PHIL: Well it annoys Johnny. But I'd also say those sentiments were disloyal, even unpatriotic, Amanda.

MANDY: Steady on, Phil.

PHIL: No, because you see, what I find really *offensive* Amanda is the imputation that, engaged as we are in a thrilling contest of sporting prowess against the Old Enemy of cricket, that you would utter such thoughts as might be called disloyal or indeed…

MANDY: Don't say it Phil…

PHIL: Well what I do find offensive is that you would impute negative thoughts against the Australian cricket team—

MANDY: But—

PHIL: In our own living room! It is unconscionable! And quite reprehensible in the extreme!

MANDY: Well, okay. [*Mischievously*] Would you say it was seditious?

PHIL: [*exasperated*] No because an utterance act made in good faith, Mandy, and not in the course of criticism of the Crown, the Governor-General, the Cabinet or the Parliament of Australia, Mandy, is not sedition, and if you'd studied law and if your father was a Liberal member you'd know like I do.

MANDY: Your Daddy is a Liberal MP?

PHIL: My father Maxwell is a distinguished and long-serving member of the House.

MANDY: You never told me that, Phil.

PHIL: I must have neglected to include a family history with my lease application.

MANDY: Christ, I hate politicians.

PHIL: There's no need to blaspheme!

MANDY: Oh grow up, Phil, this isn't your daddy's office anymore.

PHIL: Well I don't accept your criticism at all and I remain certain of my certainty of being right.

> MANDY *doesn't reply, and just laughs and shakes her head.*

And furthermore I'm taking steps—

> *But he gets interrupted by* JOHNNY *entering with three beers.*

What's this?

> JOHNNY *comes back into the living room jovially carrying three beers:*

JOHNNY: Now fellas, oh sorry Mandy, now, er, comrades—

PHIL: I am not your comrade, John, that is what Communists and... [*He shudders.*] trade unionists call each other.

JOHNNY: Yeah, ah, sorry fellas, okay so cheers.

> *They clink.* JOHNNY *sits down on the couch, and the others eventually follow.* JOHNNY *swigs from his beer.*

Ah, that's better. You had me quite worked up there for a second, Mandy.

MANDY: Warney's fighting back.

JOHNNY: Ah yes, I knew he'd come through for Australia. He's the most patriotic of the team you know Mandy, actually definitely the leader in the dressing-room and they say apparently Ponting's chief tactician...

PHIL: I never cared too much for Shane Warne. He always offended my sensibilities. I have always preferred the metronomic accuracy of Glen McGrath.

MANDY: Ohh-ahh, Glen McGrath.

JOHNNY: Yes we need him to stay fit all series! That's for sure. [*Snarling*] C'mon Warney!

PHIL: Well I hate to interrupt this little sporting occasion but I am going back to study for my law exams.

MANDY: Go Phil!

JOHNNY: Oh stay and drink your beer Phil. Don't be such a tight-arse.

PHIL: Again, I believe I am thoroughly justified when I say I have reason for showing grievance at the level of abuse in this living room!

MANDY: [*pointing at* JOHNNY] Oh you should have seen him earlier Phil, he was being the biggest cunt.

PHIL: Yes, I can rather imagine, Amanda. No doubt John you were showing your customary combativeness combined with a certain malleable relationship to the truth?

JOHNNY: I do not have to sit here and listen to this while I'm trying to watch the cricket.

MANDY: This isn't cricket, this is a Shane Warne hair replacement ad!

JOHNNY: But the abuse! The abuse in my own living room, while the cricket is on!

PHIL: Yes, it's amazing how you put up with loud sporting fixtures in the living room while other members of the household are trying to better themselves—

MANDY: You're not fucking bettering yourself! Your daddy was a lawyer too!

PHIL: [*continuing with his speech*] Trying to better themselves by defending their top marks in the subject.

MANDY: All while Warney's talking to Gooch about hair replacement.

JOHNNY: Well perhaps you should think about it, Phil. Getting a bit thin on top there mate.

PHIL: It is not.

JOHNNY: It is too!

PHIL: It is not getting, as you say, *thin* on top. And really, any criticism in this respect from you John I find highly hypocritical.

MANDY: *Highly* hypocritical.

The cricket is back on; Warne hits a four in the television commentary.

ALL: Yeah!

JOHNNY: Warney!

PHIL: Yes, it's all very stimulating but I'm off to study.

JOHNNY: Well mate, enjoy that study, I can't understand it myself but respect to you for sticking with your hard work.

PHIL: I will. Call me if you need me.

> PHIL *exits.*

JOHNNY: Well if we have any crises I'll give you a yell, Phil.

MANDY: Warne gone.

JOHNNY: Arrrgggghhh!

SCENE SIX

ASIF *enters through the front door.*

MANDY: Who the *fuck* are you?

> *She scrambles to put away the bong.* ASIF *stands bewildered, just inside the front door, looking at the strange new lounge-room in which he has just arrived.*

JOHNNY: [*stands up*] G'day mate, what can I do for you?

ASIF: I would like to apply for asylum.

MANDY: What the fuck—are you talking about?

JOHNNY: Ah, I think you've got the wrong place mate. This is not—

ASIF: My name is Asif Muhammed al-Suhail and I wish to apply for asylum.

> MANDY *jumps off the couch and hides behind the couch near* JOHNNY.

MANDY: Did you hear that?

JOHNNY: Yeah—now this is not—

MANDY: Did you hear that? Did you hear what he just said?

JOHNNY: Now, hang on—

MANDY: Who is he?

JOHNNY: Mandy—

ASIF: Excuse me. I wish to apply for asylum.

MANDY: This is not an asylum!

JOHNNY: [*to* MANDY] Calm down!

MANDY: What if he's like a terrorist or something?

JOHNNY: Just calm down!

ASIF: I am making an official request for asylum.

JOHNNY: You pipe down too!

MANDY: He's a fucking Al Qaeda terrorist Johnny, he's going to kill us all!

ASIF: I am asking for your help.

JOHNNY: Now look mate, I think you've got the wrong house.

MANDY: Are you a terrorist?

ASIF: No! I haven't hurt anyone.

JOHNNY: How'd you get here?

ASIF: I crossed the road, the big road.

JOHNNY: What?

ASIF: From the house, where I stay. I had to leave. Please. I am asking you for asylum.

JOHNNY: Mate you can't be a refugee from a *house*. It doesn't work like that.

MANDY: Yeah, you have to be from a *country*!

ASIF: But the police—

JOHNNY: What's this about the police?

ASIF: The police, they raided our house. Everyone evicted.

JOHNNY: Now steady on. I know plenty of cops. They wouldn't do that for no reason. If they raided your house, they must have known you were doing something wrong.

ASIF: No! No. [*He begins to cry.*] I am sorry.

Long pause, punctuated by ASIF*'s sobs.*

MANDY: Well, he can't stay here—

JOHNNY: Well, I know he can't.

ASIF: Please. I am sorry. Will you let me stay?

JOHNNY *walks to the door and looks outside. He looks around the door landing, inspecting* ASIF, *who is still crying on the floor.*

JOHNNY: Where did he fucking come from?

MANDY: [*still hiding the bong behind the couch*] He can't stay, Johnny, no fucking way!

JOHNNY: No well I agree about that Mandy, we just have to work out what to do with him.

ASIF: Please, I ask you, human being to human being, for help.

JOHNNY: Oh for Chrissake.

ASIF: Grant me asylum. Let me stay here. I must find a job.

JOHNNY: That's not my problem, mate, I'm sorry.

ASIF: You do not perhaps understand. I cannot find a job—

JOHNNY: Oh mate, don't give me that bullshit. In this country, anyone who wants to work can get a job.

ASIF: I have heard this: but it is not true.

JOHNNY: Right: see, the thing is mate, I'm not the stinking government. I only run a servo down the road. Mandy might know a bit more about this; she works at Centrelink.

MANDY: I stamp the forms, John.

JOHNNY: Well, and you see, that's the problem. We [*looking to* MANDY, *then back to* ASIF.] can't help you with asylum. Maybe you need to talk to the police.

ASIF: Oh, God, no, please, not again.

MANDY: No cops, Johnny. [*In a stage whisper*] They'll find the fucking stash.

ASIF: [*going to* JOHNNY *and holding him*] Please, you must help me. Help me find a safe place.

JOHNNY: I just told you mate. I can't help you. Look, there's the Kiwis over the road.

ASIF: [*still holding on*] No, not over the road. I have come so far, you do not understand—no-one will help me. Please help me sir!

JOHNNY: [*struggling with* ASIF, *batting him down*] Now just—steady—on mate.

ASIF: I want only your help for a short time—

MANDY: Go on Johnny—tell him to get out!

> ASIF *takes the opportunity to try and hug* JOHNNY *tightly around his waist.*

JOHNNY: Steady on mate!

> JOHNNY, *startled, heaves* ASIF *off him, throwing him against the wall, where he hits his head and falls motionless on the floor.*

Oh for fuck's sake, now look what you made me do Mandy, I've gone and hurt the little bastard.

MANDY: Ohmigod John, are you alright?

JOHNNY: Yeah, I'm alright, Mandy. Old mate might have a sore head tomorrow though.

MANDY: Don't blame me, Johnny, you're the one who's bashed his head against the wall.

JOHNNY: Well fair enough too, we're not a home for the poor. I mean we don't even know who he is. I bet he's not really from over the road at all.

MANDY: Well let's hope he bloody wakes up, or we might never know. [*Pause.*] What are we going to do?

JOHNNY: We'll work something out.

MANDY: No, I mean, if he doesn't wake up.

JOHNNY: Self-defence, Mandy, you said it yourself.

JOHNNY *gets up from the couch and walks over to* ASIF, *who lies where he fell. Cautiously,* JOHNNY *gives him a nudge with his shoe. No response.* JOHNNY *nudges harder. No response.* JOHNNY *gives him a short kick, then a harder one.* ASIF *recoils sharply, and moans.*

Yeah, he's alright.

JOHNNY *picks* ASIF *up and drags him to the cupboard door. He moans but doesn't move much or resist.* JOHNNY *laboriously holds the cupboard door open with one foot while dragging* ASIF *inside. He drops him inside the cupboard with a loud thud.*

MANDY: What are you doing?

JOHNNY: Putting him into detention. While we figure out what the fuck we're supposed to do.

MANDY: Is he… okay? I'm sorry, I'm really worried that you've hurt him badly.

JOHNNY: Now listen to me, Mandy, you better back me up on this—

MANDY: I'm not backing anyone up, Johnny, I did not bash this man over the head—

JOHNNY: Yeah well he attacked me, didn't he, so it served him right. Stupid fucking refo, he deserves what he gets. [*Long pause.*] Christ, after all that I need another beer. Do you want one Mandy?

MANDY *doesn't reply.*

JOHNNY: Mandy? [*No reply.*] *Mandy!*

MANDY: What?

JOHNNY: Doesn't matter. I'm going to get myself another beer.

> JOHNNY *exits to the kitchen. He returns promptly with another beer. There is a long pause after he opens it, while* JOHNNY *and* MANDY *look at each other. Eventually cricket commentary returns.*

SCENE SEVEN

PHIL *enters.*

PHIL: What seems to be the issue here?

JOHNNY: It's okay, Phil, we're handling this.

MANDY: John's bashed a homeless man against the wall—

PHIL: Is that so, John?

JOHNNY: No it is not, Phil. We had a bit of home invasion, that's what we had.

MANDY: Some little Arab bloke from across the suburb's come over to talk to us, and Johnny's bashed him against the wall and now he's knocked out.

JOHNNY: Oh cheers, Mandy, I appreciate your support.

PHIL: Well, ahem, where is this alleged home invader?

JOHNNY: He's in the cupboard.

PHIL: Ah John, why is he in the cupboard?

JOHNNY: Because I bloody well put him there! [*Pause.*] It was self-defence; Mandy said it herself.

MANDY: He could have been telling the truth, you didn't have to bash him.

JOHNNY: Well I think he should have thought about that before he came cap in hand asking for bloody asylum.

PHIL: Asylum? Indeed?

JOHNNY: [*self-assured*] It's okay Phil, I've sorted it, I've locked him in the cupboard.

MANDY: Well he can't stay there, Johnny, he's got to go.

PHIL: Oh look, Gilchrist out.

JOHNNY: Look, this is no time for cricket scores Phil, even I can see that. There's a potential terrorist in the house and we need to come up with a plan.

PHIL: Well, where he is now?

JOHNNY: Everything's all right now, I've locked him in the cupboard.

PHIL: So you said.

JOHNNY: Yeah, that's right.

MANDY: Do you think he's safe in the cupboard Johnny?

JOHNNY: I expect he's very safe. [*Walking over to the cupboard.*] Oi! You okay?

> ASIF *murmers inaudibly and the sound of scraping emerges from the cupboard.*

I said, *are you okay?* [*Looking back at the TV screen to see the replay of Gilchrist's dismissal*] Oh for Chrissake's Gilly, what sort of shot was that?

PHIL: Did he, ahem, identify himself as a refugee? That could be an important legal distinction.

MANDY: He said something about an asylum. And told his name, but I couldn't understand it.

JOHNNY: I remember it, it was Sohail, um, yeah, Javed Miandad Sohail.

ASIF: Help! Help me! Let me out!

JOHNNY: [*banging on the cupboard door*] Shut up you fucking towel-head. Now listen. Phil, what are we going to do with him?

PHIL: We could try calling the police.

MANDY: No cops, Phil! I'd have to get rid of me bong and all me buds. Fuck that. No cops.

PHIL: Another reason, if one were needed, to quit that filthy habit, Mandy.

JOHNNY: Right, Phil, you're the lawyer, what are we going to do?

PHIL: Ahem, well how did you manage to attack him and lock him the cupboard John? I would advise you not to attack the legalities if you are remanded in custody on assault charges.

JOHNNY: Yeah well that's why I'm asking you, Phil, *what are we doing to do?*

PHIL: Created a bit of a situation for ourselves, have we? Ahem. Hmmm.

Let me see. I propose that we adjourn discussions for a few overs until we can quorum on an appropriate solution.

JOHNNY: And what exactly is that Phil? This 'quorum' of yours?

PHIL: Well, it often eventuates that a decision reached in haste can lead to unforeseen consequences, the adverse effects of which could be avoided if due care and diligence were exercised in the fullness of time and in the appropriate climate of careful deliberation. Also, I believe that Lee and Warne are making a late-order stand and it would be remiss of us, John, not to lend them our support in this troubled time for the Australian middle-order.

JOHNNY: Well said young Phillip, let's get you another beer.

JOHNNY *exits.*

MANDY: Look, Phil, we can't just lock this person up like that. Isn't there—

PHIL: But, ah, ahem, Amanda, I thought you believed he was—and still may be—a, how shall we say it, potential suspect in the war on terror.

MANDY: Well Phil I think you should know this, I think Johnny's hurt the little bugger actually. He's not making a lot of noise from that cupboard.

PHIL: Injured him?

MANDY: That's right, Phil, he bashed his head against the wall. He's left a bloody mark.

PHIL: I don't think he would have hurt his head too badly. It's a very thin wall that, I should know, I have to study behind it while you and Johnny carry on like a married couple. And another thing, Mandy, any damage that this terrorist has done will certainly be taken up with him before he leaves, I'm not letting an Islamist ruin my bond!

MANDY: Couldn't it be there's perhaps a law, a general *rule*, y'know, against locking people in the cupboard when they ask you for help? It's a bit of a concern isn't it, Phil?

PHIL: What's more concerning, Amanda, is, ahem, your attitude towards this 'guest' as you call him, this in fact *uninvited* guest, this un-asked-for cupboard dweller. It is in fact the fact that this character, well it's a *non-permitted* threshold crossing, it's in fact an unscheduled non-certified unofficial living room inspection, and I argue Mandy that this fellow is indeed a *home invader*! There is a process for coming into this house Mandy, an orderly process, and you can't just jump the queue.

MANDY: Phil, I don't reckon there's ever been a queue at the door to our house.

PHIL: You may be forgetting the, ahem, karaoke party, in which John's rendition of 'Khe Sanh' brought quite a number of guests who arrived all at once.

MANDY: It was the cops, Phil.

PHIL: That, I think, is precisely my *point*. The fact is that by coming into our house without being invited, on no official business, without credentials of any kind, without any attempt to respect or maintain the integrity of the borders of our property, he is taking the place of other guests who might legitimately want to come and visit us and stay in our closet. I am well aware of our international obligations in regards to the rights of the closet, extremely aware, Amanda, and I'm not going to stand for it.

MANDY: Phil, you may have missed an important point of mine here: what if he's hurt? What are we going to do about him now? We can't ask him to leave if he's unconscious.

PHIL: Well that's precisely correct, Mandy, and it is exactly this sort of thing that makes these people so dangerous. You let them into your home and before you know they've barricaded themselves in the cupboard and started a consciousness strike. I tell you now Mandy, we are not going to give in to this kind of intimidation!

JOHNNY *enters, carrying beers.*

JOHNNY: Too right mate, I've been thinking: we can't be letting just anyone in here, not during the Ashes. It spoils the enjoyment for everyone.

PHIL: John, I believe we need to conference on this.

JOHNNY *opens a beer, hands it to* PHIL, *and they clink.* JOHNNY *takes a swig and lets out a loud exhalation of beery contentment.*

JOHNNY: Ahhh. Now that's a conference.

MANDY: Did you get a chance to *think* about what we might do with the person that we *did* let in, and that you, like, bashed the crap out of?

JOHNNY: Well, that's an unsubstantiated rumour, based on hearsay, isn't it, Phil?

PHIL: Quite.

JOHNNY: Would you describe it as un-Australian, Phil? Rumours of that kind?

PHIL: I'm afraid that a reasonable person would have no choice but to do so.

JOHNNY: See? Phil's going to work all this out, aren't you mate?

PHIL: Yes, yes I am. I am going to consult the relevant household regulations and I'll let you know after the fall of the next wicket.

JOHNNY: That's a good boy.

> PHIL *exits.*

You know, Mandy, sometimes I reckon Phil's not so bad.

MANDY: Sure.

JOHNNY: I'm going to get another beer. And see if I can pick Phil's brains. Ah, call me if there's a wicket will you Mandy?

> *He exits.*

Oh, and ah, don't let old mate out of the cupboard.

SCENE EIGHT

ASIF: Hello?

> MANDY *hears but says nothing.*

Hello? Is there anyone out there?

MANDY: Shhh.

ASIF: Hello? Hello? [*Knocking and scraping on the cupboard door*] Who is there?

MANDY: Shoosh.

ASIF: Hello?

MANDY: Shoosh!

ASIF: Who is there?

MANDY: Shut up.

ASIF: Hello?

MANDY: Listen mate, you need to be quiet.

ASIF: Hello? Who is there? Can you let me out please?

MANDY: Well I don't know whether I should.

ASIF: Hello?

MANDY: Listen mate, if Johnny or Phil hear you and come back in here—

ASIF: Let me out please! Please, let me out!

He knocks loudly on the cupboard door.

MANDY: Fuck. [*Getting up and walking quickly over to the cupboard.*] Quiet. Just be quiet. What are you doing here?

ASIF: My name is Asif Muhammed al-Suhail and I wish to apply for asylum.

MANDY: Yes, I heard you say that. But there are some things I need to know.

ASIF: Can I come out, please?

MANDY: I don't think that's a good idea.

ASIF: Are you police?

MANDY: No, I'm not the police.

ASIF: Why am I locked up here?

MANDY: Look, you…

Pause.

ASIF: Why am I locked up in this place?

MANDY: We weren't expecting you.

ASIF: I have had a house, you know. I have had a house, and when I had a house, with my family, and we had a guest arrive, uninvited, it is customary to serve *tea*.

MANDY: Well, *fuck you*.

ASIF: What? I am sorry. [*He knocks again.*] Please. I am sorry.

MANDY: *Better* than us now, are ya?

ASIF: I did not mean to offend you. I am locked in a cupboard. I am trying to make a joke. I am sorry.

MANDY: What'd you say?

ASIF: I said I was sorry.

Pause.

MANDY: How are you feeling?

ASIF: I feel bad.

MANDY: How bad?

ASIF· I don't know.

MANDY: Look, if I—let you out, will you promise me to be very quiet?

ASIF: Yes.

> MANDY *opens the door and* ASIF *emerges.*

MANDY: Are you okay?

ASIF: My head hurts.

MANDY: Bloody Johnny. I'll get you some ice.

> MANDY *exits.* ASIF *touches his head wound experimentally and winces.* MANDY *comes back with a bag of frozen peas.*

Put this on your head.

ASIF: It's cold.

MANDY: It'll help with the bruising. Here—sit down…

ASIF: Thank you—Mandy?

MANDY: Yeah. Yeah. Right. So. Why are you here? Why did you come here?

ASIF: I have nowhere else I can go.

MANDY: Right. See, that's not true.

ASIF: No, it is true.

MANDY: There are three dozen houses in this street. There's a whole *suburb*—

ASIF: You are Australian—yes? You are sharing a house? Students? Young people?

MANDY: Look, we're not bloody hippies, mate, alright? We don't just let all comers crash on the couch. We're working people.

ASIF: You work…?

MANDY: *Yes*—what, women don't work where you come from?

ASIF: No, I mean, do you work tomorrow?

> MANDY *doesn't reply, but looks at him questionably.*

Do I disturb you?

MANDY: Well, yes, you do, you have, but no, I'm not working tomorrow, since you ask, it's Sunday.

ASIF: I also want to work, you see. I am a computer programmer.

MANDY: Really.

ASIF: Oracle PQ/SQL database. I was trained in Dubai.

MANDY: Right. The thing is that you can't stay here.

ASIF: But I am here.

MANDY: Yes, and the thing is that you have to leave.

ASIF: I—how do I explain? I am a human being. You are a human being. I do not hurt you. I come to you for help. I ask you for your help as a human being.

MANDY: And I tell you that I can't help you.

ASIF: But it is not true.

MANDY: Or I could just not argue this and say that I couldn't be bothered, and that if you don't leave I'll get Johnny back in here and let him know you tried to *rape* me. How about that? [*Pause.*] Look, you scared me, alright? In fact, you really haven't stopped scaring me. Because I don't know who you are.

ASIF: I am a man who is asking you for help.

MANDY: I can't help you.

ASIF: One night only. So I can sleep. Please. I cannot make sense of the world like this. This is a bad dream.

MANDY: Why should I help you?

ASIF: Because we are children of God, both of us.

> MANDY *opens her mouth and nothing comes out.*

Just help me stay for a night.

JOHNNY: [*offstage*] Mandy, do you want another beer?

MANDY: [*to* ASIF] Get back in the cupboard.

ASIF: Just one night.

MANDY: Get back in the cupboard now. If you say one word to them— *one word*—I will let them do what they want to you. Bad things. Do you understand? *Do you understand?*

> ASIF *nods.*

Get back in the cupboard and I'll see what I can do.

> ASIF *does so.*

> *The cricket commentary drones on long enough to let* MANDY *return to the couch, where she visibly composes herself. It drones on long enough, even, for* MANDY *to pack another cone.*

SCENE NINE

JOHNNY *enters.*

JOHNNY: I got you a beer anyway.

MANDY: Thanks.

JOHNNY: Lost any wickets?

MANDY: Nope.

JOHNNY: I knew it! Bretty Lee fights back!

MANDY: Uh huh.

JOHNNY: 'What ocean's name means "peaceful"?'

MANDY: What?

JOHNNY: 'What ocean's name means "peaceful"?'

MANDY: What?

JOHNNY: 'Pacific'. The Pacific Ocean. You know that?

MANDY: Yeah, I think I did actually.

JOHNNY: Fuckin' hell. [*He puts the bottle cap down.*] They should stick to questions about sport over at CUB I reckon. You alright?

MANDY: Yep.

JOHNNY: Did he say something to you?

MANDY: Nup.

> PHIL *enters.*

JOHNNY: Right. Phil. The lawyer. What are we going to do?

PHIL: Ahem, well, after perusing the relevant section of the act dealing with Household Home Invasions During The Ashes Series, I believe I have come up with a fair and equitable solution for all parties, one that safeguards our home's cupboard security as well as guaranteeing the right of our interloper to leave.

JOHNNY: Bonza! Ah… what is it?

PHIL: Ahem, well, I propose that for the purposes of this Ashes Series, we adopt what might be termed a fairly radical solution, but nevertheless, I think we'll find, one that's legally watertight, and maintains the integrity of… [*He spreads his hands.*] Our way of life.

MANDY: And what is it, Phil?

PHIL: Having obtained a copy of the lease and the relevant Act…

JOHNNY: Yeah…?

PHIL: I took the liberty of calling our landlord earlier—

MANDY: It's 10 o'clock at night.

PHIL: Well it just so happens that my father knows the real estate agent's wife, she's a stalwart of the local branch, and so I was able to contact her at this late instance, knowing as I do [*he chuckles*] that she's a religious watcher of 'Lateline'—

MANDY: 'Lateline'?

PHIL: Yes, 'Lateline'.

MANDY: I like his ties.

PHIL: Tony Jones is a raving ABC Socialist Amanda. However, be that as it may, his taste in neckwear seems to have put our Grace in a generous mood, and through her I've been able to contact our landlord, and we have been able, successfully, to excise this closet from the lease.

    Pause.

JOHNNY: Right. That's… sorry, I don't get it.

PHIL: The *Residential Tenancies Act* is quite clear on this. It correlates, interestingly enough, with statutes at every relevant legislative level. Quite extraordinary, really.

MANDY: What does it *say*…?

PHIL: The Act states that we have no responsibility to look after him if he's not on our property. Therefore I propose that we excise the cupboard from the lease, for the purposes of being able to refuse responsibility for [*to* JOHNNY] not only for the thrashing he appears already to have received, but for his physical well-being *prior, during* and *following* his 'request', which is now, legally, rendered null and void, in that there is no legal basis for it to have happened at all.

MANDY: How did he get into the cupboard?

PHIL: I'm sorry?

MANDY: The cupboard's still in the house. To get into it he must have come through the property—

PHIL: Speaking as an advocate, I wouldn't like to have to prove that. There's a whole chain of hearsay to trip you up there.

JOHNNY: I'm sorry—you're gonna have to explain this again, Phil.

PHIL: This man is Not Our Problem Anymore.

JOHNNY: Really.

PHIL: Yes.

JOHNNY: You beauty. [*To* MANDY] See? I told you living with a law student was a good idea.

MANDY: Yeah, that's great, Phil. And what about the others?

PHIL: What others?

MANDY: Now don't get me wrong—

JOHNNY: Mandy, what exactly is your fucking problem?

MANDY: The problem is this, John. He found us. He got himself here. Or was brought. By person or persons unknown. Apparently we're a soft touch.

PHIL: Perhaps he spied your water pipe through the front window, Amanda, and mistook this for a house of left-wing time-wasters.

JOHNNY: Yeah? I'll show anybody just who is and isn't a fuckin' soft touch around here mate.

He slams a fist into his palm and laughs. He calls into the cupboard.

Eh mate? Eh Javed? Would you say I'm a soft touch mate?

MANDY: Yeah. Right. The thing is, John, that you bashing the shit out of him is about the *least* helpful thing that could possibly have happened. The fact that he's in the cupboard and that Phil has come up with—and I'm not saying it's not ingenious—but it's a stupid plan.

PHIL: And may I ask *what* your basis for this assessment might be, Amanda, from, ahem, Centrelink?

JOHNNY: Heh heh heh.

MANDY: How many cupboards do you think we *have?*

JOHNNY: There's this one, and the one in the other room.

MANDY: And what are we going to do after that? After we've filled every cupboard, closet and pantry in the place and *excised* them all from the *lease*? What do we do then?

JOHNNY: Mandy, alright, you're losing it here, mate. Chances are, by that time, the Ashes'll be over, and…

MANDY: And what…?

PHIL: What do you, ahem, propose as an alternative…?

MANDY: Like I was saying, Phil, it's not that it's a bad *idea* you've had, it's that it's not much of a *plan*. And what I think we should do is something a bit more *radical*.

PHIL: Well, Amanda, I have to say, I'm all ears.

JOHNNY: Shit, me too. [*To TV*] Ooohrr, fuck that was close! Jeez that reverse swing's a fucking *killer*. C'mon Bretty Lee! Keep your head son! Keep your head!

MANDY: I think the solution has to be to relocate him.

JOHNNY: Well, I think that's a job for the police and the relevant authorities, and now that our responsibility has been shifted by the excision of the cupboard from the—

MANDY: Well, I think that's where you're wrong. This is our problem. We're letting *other people* determine where our house begins and ends. What our responsibilities are. There's only one way to stop that. We've gotta take a stand.

JOHNNY: I don't reckon that's up to us.

MANDY: Don't ya. Take a look at Brett Lee. What's he doing? Is he complaining that it's not his job to bat Australia out of trouble? No. He's stepping up to the crease. He's doing what he has to do.

PHIL: Yes, Amanda, that's all very well, but how and where exactly do you propose to 'relocate' him?

MANDY: Well, it's funny—it just so happens that there's a particular island, here, let me show you— [*She pulls a refidex from under the couch and leafs through it*] whose residents, man, woman and child, without exception, depend fortnightly upon a particular stamp from a particular office which neither of you boys are very familiar with, of course, but believe me when I say, they are *not* busy.

JOHNNY: Why would we send him to an island full of dole bludgers? Sounds like a holiday.

MANDY: Well, I don't want to look after him, you don't want to look after him, Phil doesn't want to look after him, but at the moment, *we are*. And you can be sure that whoever sent him here *sees that*. So we gotta send a message. Trust me. Once word gets out about our solution, we'll have the most peaceful Ashes series in living memory.

JOHNNY: Ahhhr the *fucking* Poms get the new ball. That's all we need.

PHIL: And how do you, ahem, propose to persuade the inhabitants of said island to participate in this little scheme, Amanda…?

MANDY: Simple. Bump the entire island to Disability Support Pension with Carer's Allowance: one stroke of a computer key, and they'll think it's bloody Christmas.

JOHNNY: Right. So once again poor old Muggins the taxpayer foots the bill for a parasite.

MANDY: Fine, John. Just let me ask you this. *Can* you, right now, can you put a dollar value on *your* peace of mind?

Pause.

JOHNNY: Well, that's a very good question, Mandy, and I'd like to remind you that I've always maintained that no price is too high to pay for the security and stability of our neighbourhood.

MANDY: There's a family who always comes to the office in a one-tonner, they got a couple of boys. Tomorrow morning, I'll give 'em a call, they'll come by and pick it up.

PHIL: Pick up…?

MANDY: The cupboard.

PHIL: The cupboard…?

MANDY: Well, it's not really ours anymore, is it, you made quite sure of that, you clever thing.

PHIL: You're going to—

MANDY *puts her finger rapidly to her lips and jerks her head toward the cupboard.* PHIL *speaks more quietly.*

Leave him in there?

MANDY: No, we're just going to let him run around wherever he wants, of course. John, could you turn the TV up a bit…? Thanks.

PHIL: I was given to understand, ahem, that the fellow in question was to be transported to a locale surrounded by a body of water.

MANDY: It's called an island, Phil, and people live there, and this bloke is still very much an unknown quantity. Not to mention what might happen to him if he goes wandering off.

PHIL: How long, um, would this period of internment be projected to last?

MANDY: As long as it takes. I mean, Phil, what you don't seem to realise is that we've got to be prepared next time. We've got to have procedures in place, or we're opening ourselves up to be manipulated—

JOHNNY: What?

MANDY: I'm saying, if we don't have a plan, we're opening ourselves up to be manipulated by any shyster who tries to persuade us, in a moment of weakness, to make ourselves the victims of our own *conscience*.

JOHNNY: Sorry?

MANDY: People will take advantage of our good nature.

JOHNNY: Yeah. *Fuck* yeah. I *hate* that. [*He yells at the cupboard*] I fucking *hate* that shit.

MANDY: See, I for one can't think of a more peaceful—a more pacific—solution to the problem.

PHIL: I find this, I have to say, this Pacific Solution to be fundamentally at odds with, uh, some basic humanitarian considerations which, as campus president of the Amnesty chapter, I find…

Beat.

MANDY: You find—what, Phil?

PHIL: I find morally objectionable.

MANDY: Do you. [*She looks at* JOHNNY] John?

JOHNNY: Yep?

MANDY: Phil's got moral objections.

JOHNNY: Really.

MANDY: See, I think that's probably best kept between us, Phil.

JOHNNY: Yeah, I reckon that's best kept under the old slouch hat, cob.

MANDY: Cause let's face it. We can't really afford to be split on this issue. It's gonna look pretty bad.

JOHNNY: Really pretty fuckin' bad. Yep, I'd say unity's the key. [*Pause.*] See, Phil, at a time like this, with Australia in trouble, y'know—[*He slaps the couch beside him: 'come sit down'*] your country needs you. Grab yourself a beer.

MANDY: And one for me, please.

JOHNNY: Actually, mate, while you're up.

PHIL *exits.*

Onya Phil. You're a trooper mate.

MANDY *comes and sits back down beside* JOHNNY.

Beer. Cones. Cricket.

He can't resist glancing at the cupboard.

MANDY: Johnny, mate? Just try and put it out of your mind. Ohhhr, there's that Pom.

JOHNNY: Flintoff. Bastard.

> *They watch intently as Flintoff bowls and Brett Lee defends deftly.*

Go Bretty Lee! Come on the late order!

MANDY: Like it never happened.

JOHNNY: What?

> *They look quickly back at the screen, where Lee and his partner have just stolen a second run.*

Go Bretty Lee! Go Australia.

MANDY: Lighter.

> JOHNNY *passes it to her.*

> *Lights down.*

THE END

HALAL el-Mashakel

LINDA JAIVIN

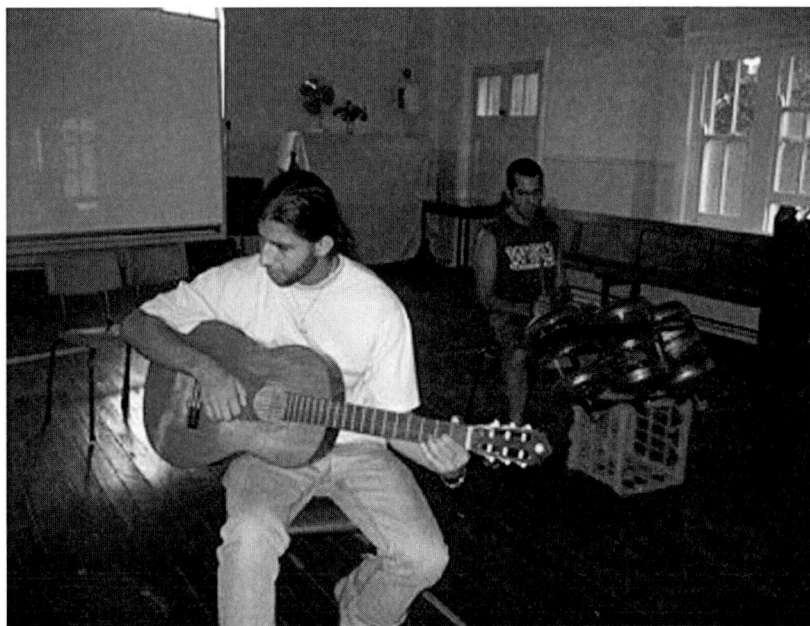

Morteza Poorvadi as Sa'id Ihram and Jared Housman as Khalil Mubarak in rehearsal for the 2004 Adelaide Fringe Festival, Adelaide. (Photo: Linda Jaivin.)

Introduction

Linda Jaivin spent an intensive period of several years visiting asylum seekers detained at western Sydney's Villawood immigration detention centre. *Halal-el-Mashakel* is one of three works that she wrote in response to this (others include her 2003 comic play, *Seeking Djira*, and her 2006 tragi-comic novel, *The Infernal Optimist*). The young protagonists in *Halal-el-Mashakel* are inspired by real people who have since been released from detention: the guitarist by Iranian (then) teenager Morteza Poorvadi, who loved playing Cat Stevens songs, and the drummer by another young man who liked music, loved drums—but hated Cat Stevens. It's a simple conceit, but an effective one, which eloquently taps into how music can be both a tool for joyful creativity *and* a means of channeling festering antagonisms and even self-destructive impulses.

Halal-el-Mashakel was first produced at the Old Fitzroy Hotel Theatre in Sydney at the start of 2003 as a double-bill with Iranian theatre practitioner and former refugee Shahin Shafaei's one-man play, *Refugitive*. The double-bill was called *Let Loose*, its tag line, 'two plays from the other side of the razor wire'. Subsequently, over a period of almost two years, the plays were presented interstate independently of each other at various fringe and festival venues. At the Adelaide Fringe in 2004, Poorvadi fulfilled his dream of acting in the play. *Halal-el-Mashakel* can be contextualised against the backdrop of a cultural upwelling in Australia of support for detained asylum seekers—and outrage at the conditions in which they were being detained—in the immediate 'post-*Tampa*' years (for a summary of the *Tampa* affair, see my introduction (p. 3) to version 1.0's *CMI*).

Jaivin presents a portrait of the psychological damage done by indefinite detention, particularly of young people. The guitarist's and the drummer's aimlessness comes literally from their increasing struggle to see anything to *aim for*, a future into which they can imaginatively project themselves. Certain characteristics of the play are Beckettian—its sparseness, its characters' submission to bewildering authority, its claustrophobic focus on two people's powerlessness to do much more

115

than narrate the passing of time. But it would be going too far to tag the pair as an Estragon and Vladimir for contemporary Australian asylum politics. The protagonists in *Halal-el-Mashakel* are experiencing a *situational* boredom more than an *existential* boredom, though the two may end up looking very similar.

A challenge for any playwright impelled by express political or ideological purposes is to avoid didacticism as well as the instrumentalisating of protagonists. Jaivin circumvents this with characters who are unremarkable, or to put it differently, who respond to remarkable circumstances in ways that any 'ordinary' person might. This includes irritable or petty behaviour, taking out frustrations on those closest, failing to share favourite snacks with a friend and so on. It also means failing at being tragic heroes; the guitarist's suicide attempt does not precipitate a conventional dramatic climax, or at least, Jaivin undercuts the climax by infusing its fallout with sly, dark humour:

> DRUMMER: But shampoo? You can't kill yourself just by drinking shampoo. Fucking idiot.
> GUITARIST: I suppose that was pretty stupid.
> DRUMMER: What next? [*A beat.*] Conditioner?
> GUITARIST: I thought maybe gel.

Jaivin commented in email correspondence with me that one of her aims in writing *Halal-el-Mashakel* was to present her characters as typical young men, rather than to imply that asylum seekers' entitlement to better treatment upon arrival in Australia is contingent upon them being 'good' or 'innocent' people:

> They are just human beings. Fucked up, smart, stupid, flawed, funny, lovely at times, horrible at others—in other words just like you and me. The victim/hero narrative tends to turn people into objects of compassion or pity on the one hand and respect and admiration on the other, but it doesn't encourage deep identification. I wanted to show that the asylum seekers are no different from us, and just as deserving of fair, just and humane treatment in accordance with the principles of human rights as the rest of us. How would two Australian teenage boys behave if they were put in a terrible situation—faced with persecution or torture—ran from it and then were locked up indefinitely for reasons that had more to do with politics than justice?

There's every chance that two young Australians would behave very much like Jaivin's guitarist and drummer and that, moreover, they would be shocked to discover the precariousness of their much-vaunted human rights.

Emma Cox

For Nashwan and Morteza, with thanks and affection; a deep bow to Humam for his stories and 'I'm not crazy, I just want my freedom'; for Wahab; Osama; and all other asylum seekers locked up in our detention centres. Freedom and peace to you all.

Halal-el-Mashakel was first produced by Pesto Manifesto at the Old Fitzroy Theatre, Sydney as part of a two-play production called *Let Loose*, opening on 13 January 2003 with the following cast and director:

DRUMMER, KHALIL MUBARAK	Hazem Shammas
GUITARIST, SA'ID IHRAM	Craig Menaud
GUARD	Luci Gleeson

Director, Jennifer Hamilton

Halal-el-Mashakel was subsequently staged in Canberra, Wollongong, Newcastle and at the Adelaide Festival Fringe, where Jennifer Hamilton directed Jared Houseman as the Drummer and Morteza Poorvadi, the young refugee who inspired the character of the Guitarist as the Guitarist.

CHARACTERS

DRUMMER, Khalil Mubarak. An angry young man in his early
twenties.
GUITARIST, Sa'id Ihram. A sad young man in his late teens.
GUARD

DESIGN AND SETTING

A room with a door and a window. A beat-up drum kit with a stool for
the DRUMMER, and another stool for the GUITARIST.

SCENE ONE

The GUITARIST *is tuning his guitar, playing chords. When the audience is seated,* DRUMMER *enters.*

DRUMMER: One two three four!

> *He begins drumming slowly.*

> GUITARIST *starts playing first few lines of 'Moonshadow' by Cat Stevens. As* GUITARIST *sings,* DRUMMER *speeds up and gets louder and more rock-like, drowning out the guitar and the singer.*

> GUITARIST *stops playing, looks at* DRUMMER.

> DRUMMER *stops playing.*

What?

GUITARIST: I can't even hear myself. And you're not playing the song.

DRUMMER: I hate that song.

GUITARIST: Yeah, well, we agreed. We'll do that one first, then we'll do one you like.

> *They start up again.* DRUMMER *again begins softly, but a few lines into the song, once again gets loud and rocks it, drowning out* GUITARIST.

> GUITARIST *stops playing, stands up and moves his stool as far away as possible from the drum kit.* DRUMMER *shrugs. They both start to play again, but obviously different songs. The drums drown out the guitar.*

[*Stopping*] Hey! Hey!

> GUITARIST *gets up, walks over and knocks on the cymbal for attention.* DRUMMER *looks up.*

DRUMMER: Now what?

GUITARIST: Why can't you use practice pads? They'll soften the sound.

DRUMMER: Don't wanna soften the sound.

GUITARIST *returns to his corner, starts playing.* DRUMMER *drowns him out. This happens a few times.*

GUITARIST: This is fucked. I don't wanna play with you any more.

DRUMMER: You've got no choice.

GUITARIST *goes to window, peers out. Pause.*

GUITARIST: I'd have a choice if I was out there.

DRUMMER: You're not. You don't have a choice.

GUITARIST: Neither do you. You could make an effort.

DRUMMER: I'm tired of making an effort.

GUITARIST: Yeah, well me too.

They return to their positions. They play different songs as loudly as they can for a few moments, then the DRUMMER *stops abruptly and dashes his sticks to the ground. He jumps up and starts pacing around.*

GUITARIST *ignores him, sings 'Moonshadow'.*

DRUMMER *slams his hand down on the neck of the guitar, making the* GUITARIST *jump.*

Cut it out. Just because you don't want to play doesn't mean I can't.

He continues to sing 'Moonshadow'.

DRUMMER: [*shouting*] I hate it here.

GUITARIST: [*sighs, stops playing*] And I love it?… I've been here longer than you, you know.

DRUMMER: I don't think so.

GUITARIST: I've been here twenty-two months, three weeks and a day. Counting Port Hedland and Woomera.

DRUMMER: I'm twenty-three months, one week and four days. Counting Christmas Island and Curtin.

GUITARIST: Not much difference, really.

DRUMMER: I know. It's fucked. [*Sits down and puts his head in his hands.*] When are we going to hear? When? When? When? When?

DRUMMER *repeats 'when' until he's just mumbling and then silent.*

GUITARIST *starts playing first few lines of 'Where do the Children Play?' by Cat Stevens.*

Inside the wire.

GUITARIST: Sorry?

DRUMMER: You asked, 'where do the children play?'

GUITARIST: Oh.

DRUMMER: Sometimes they stop playing completely.

He stands up.

GUITARIST: I know. I know. Do you think I don't know?

DRUMMER: Do you think *they* know?

GUITARIST: Who?

DRUMMER: [*gesturing towards audience*] Them. Outside the wire.

GUITARIST: I dunno. Ask 'em yourself.

DRUMMER: [*shouting*] Do you know? Do you? Do you? Do you?

A beat.

See? No answer. [*A beat*] In my country we say, 'When the people on the top of the mountain look at the people in the valley, they look small. But when the people in the valley look at the people on the mountain they look small to them as well'. My question is, do the people in the valley see us at all? Maybe we're so small we're invisible?

GUITARIST *strums angrily. It sounds quite rock. The* DRUMMER *listens, picks up his sticks and starts to play, then throws his sticks down again. He pulls a pack of cigarettes out of his pocket and walks over to the* GUITARIST, *offers him one. They light up and smoke in silence for a moment.* GUITARIST *chokes on the smoke, makes a face and stubs out the cigarette.*

You've got to learn how to smoke. Smoking's good.

GUITARIST: [*still coughing*] What's so good about it?

DRUMMER: Kills time.

GUITARIST: I hate that expression. Why do we have to kill time?

DRUMMER: Because otherwise time will kill us. Better to get in first.

GUITARIST: Well… playing music together kills time.

DRUMMER: Too much effort.

GUITARIST: My mother says it's important to make an effort. Or we'll end up like that Sri Lankan guy, or that Vietnamese woman.

DRUMMER: Which Vietnamese woman?

GUITARIST: The pretty one with the long hair. The one who hanged herself a couple of months ago.

DRUMMER: Oh. I thought you meant the other one. The one who slit her wrists.

GUITARIST: Either, really.

A beat.

DRUMMER: At least they managed to do away with themselves quickly. Not like that Sri Lankan dude. Stupid bastard.

GUITARIST: I don't like thinking about that.

DRUMMER: It was a hot night.

GUITARIST: I was lying on my bed, trying to read.

DRUMMER: Habib, Salim and I were watching the video of *Shrek*.

GUITARIST: Didn't have much concentration though.

DRUMMER: It was the fourth time I'd seen it.

GUITARIST: My eyes ran down the words on the page five times before I took them in.

DRUMMER: Habib said three times was enough for him. He wanted to see *Superman*, but Leila and Ameera had it.

GUITARIST: I put down the book and picked up a car magazine some visitors brought. It's easier to look at pictures.

DRUMMER: We were still arguing when there was this huge commotion.

GUITARIST: Suddenly all the guards were on their walkie-talkies.

DRUMMER: The detainees were shouting.

GUITARIST: I jumped off my bed.

DRUMMER: I ran outside.

GUITARIST: Saw he'd slashed himself all over with a razor blade.

DRUMMER: Blood everywhere.

GUITARIST: The noise woke my little sister. She saw it too.

DRUMMER: I didn't think he'd make it.

GUITARIST: Gave her nightmares for weeks. She still screams at night.

DRUMMER: But he did make it. Poor bastard.

Pause.

GUITARIST: I heard Hossein's refusing to take his medicine again. He was yelling at the doctor, 'I'm not crazy! I just want my freedom!'

DRUMMER: I'm with him.

He gets up, goes to drum kit, bangs on it for a moment.

GUITARIST: My mother tried to talk him into taking the medicine. She says try and stay sane any way you can. She says if we stay sane we win.

DRUMMER: Do you think so? Look at Ahmad. Sanest person I know. But he's been here three years. And he's lost every appeal, they won't give him a visa and they won't send him home. You think he's won? Anyway, at least you've got your mother here.

GUITARIST: So?

DRUMMER: So. You do and I don't. I don't even have a mother any more. Why couldn't she keep her mouth shut after they took my father away? She should've thought about what would happen to us.

GUITARIST: Yeah, well, I'm sorry. But stop acting like it's my fault. Like I did something wrong.

DRUMMER: If you haven't done anything wrong, tell me, why the hell are you locked up here? [*Shouting*] Why? I'll tell you what you did wrong, what we all did wrong. We came to this country in the first place!

GUITARIST turns away, picks up guitar, drags stool as far as possible away from DRUMMER and starts playing chords.

Couldn't the people smuggler have taken me to Europe? England. Germany. Even the moon would've been better. Instead, he got me to Indonesia and put me on a boat for Australia. What a fuckup. The boat was leaky and Australia watertight. If the sun had to apply for asylum, they wouldn't let light into this country.

A long pause.

GUITARIST: How long did it take you to come across?

DRUMMER: Four days. You?

GUITARIST: Five. See any sharks?

DRUMMER: Yeah. [*Stands up, mimes the story as he tells it*] This big one follows us all evening. In the middle of the night I need to have a piss. The boat's packed, and I have to pick my way through all the sleeping bodies to the stern. It's a dark night. No moon. We're moving pretty fast. There's this woman lying at the back. I take a big step to clear her and as I'm coming down on my front foot I realise I'm stepping on air. In that second I have an extremely clear vision of that shark waiting for me with its big mouth wide open for a *halal* treat. This Afghani guy is squatting nearby having a smoke. He reaches out and grabs me by the wrist as I'm about to fall into the water.

GUITARIST: Lucky!

DRUMMER: That's me. A real lucky guy. Just look at me now. Mr Good Luck himself. I wish I'd fallen off the boat there and then.

GUITARIST: So, did you piss?

DRUMMER: The Afghani guy is still holding me, right? He says, 'Go ahead. I've got you.' By now I'm too embarrassed. 'The wind,' I say. 'It'll blow onto you,' I say. He licks a finger on his other hand and holds it up. 'No,' he says. 'Wind's right. It'll blow in the other direction.'

GUITARIST: So did it?

DRUMMER: No. Poor guy.

GUITARIST: Ha!

GUARD: [*off stage*] Oi! Muster!

> GUITARIST *and* DRUMMER *walk to the door, open it. The* GUARD *is standing there with a clipboard.*

GUITARIST: [*shows ID card to* GUARD] Sa'id Ihram.

> GUARD *ticks name off list.*

DRUMMER: [*shows ID card to* GUARD] Khalil Mubarak.

> GUARD *ticks name off list.*

GUARD: You boys keeping yourselves out of trouble?

> GUITARIST *and* DRUMMER *nod.* GUARD *exits.*

> *They close the door, sit back down on their stools.*

DRUMMER: [*imitating* GUARD] 'You boys keeping yourselves out of trouble?'

> *Pause.*

GUITARIST: You know what this place feels like? An airport where the planes come and go, but all the passengers have lost their passports and are stuck in transit. Every so often, an official comes along to check your ticket. You hold your breath cuz there's a possibility that they're gonna either put you on a plane out or let you enter the country. But most of the time they're just checking to make sure you're still there, still in the transit lounge.

DRUMMER: [*angrily, rising from stool and approaching* GUITARIST] They don't have prison guards at airports.

> GUITARIST *turns his full attention back to his playing as though he hasn't heard what the* DRUMMER *said.*

They don't push you into walls at airports. They don't treat you like a fucking animal at airports.

> GUITARIST *pretends to be absorbed in playing.* DRUMMER *gets louder and closer and more insistent.*

They don't put handcuffs on you at airports! They don't beat you up at airports! They don't break your nose at airports! They don't put you into punishment cells at airports!

> GUITARIST *stops playing, puts his hands over his ears.*

[*No longer shouting*] Sorry.

GUITARIST: Leave me alone!

DRUMMER: I said I'm sorry.

GUITARIST: Go to hell.

DRUMMER: I'm already in hell.

GUITARIST: It was me that got beat up, not you. It was my fucking nose.

> GUITARIST *strums and sings, defiantly.*

> DRUMMER *sits down and drums softly and to the beat of the song for a few bars.* GUITARIST *stops.*

I might be released today. They told my family we should hear any day now. Yes, they could release me today.

DRUMMER: Don't kid yourself. They wouldn't let in sunshine, they wouldn't release a fart. If the Minister accidentally locked himself up in here he wouldn't give himself a visa to get out.

GUITARIST: Why can't I hope?

DRUMMER: Hope is useless. No. It's more than useless. It's cruel.

GUITARIST: Hope is life.

DRUMMER: What kind of life?

GUITARIST: Hope lifts you up.

DRUMMER: So it can slam you down.

GUITARIST: Without hope, this life is nothing.

DRUMMER: Face the facts. It *is* nothing.

> GUITARIST *puts down his guitar with a faraway look. Absently, he pushes up his sleeve, and traces scars on his wrist from a suicide attempt.*

DRUMMER: I didn't mean… I'm sorry…

GUITARIST: [*picks up guitar, strums, puts it down*] Sometimes, a quick death has its attractions. It's better than letting them slowly squeeze the life out of us, drop by drop.

DRUMMER: Now you're sounding like me.

GUARD: [*off stage*]… Report to the office.

DRUMMER: Who? Who'd they call?

GUITARIST: Shh!

GUARD: [*off stage*] Muhammed Sultan. Report to the office immediately. Muhammed Sultan. Report to the office immediately.

> *Pause.*

GUITARIST: What would be the first thing you'd do if you were released?

DRUMMER: Get a good meal. Real food. You?

GUITARIST: I'd go to the beach and look at the ocean. Then I want to turn my back on the ocean and look at the land.

DRUMMER: [*laughing*] You really are a funny one. But I'm serious about the food thing. I'm so fed up with the slop they serve here. You know how last night they told us we were getting a treat? Chinese food?

GUITARIST: Yeah. It was disgusting.

DRUMMER: Exactly. I thought Chinese food was supposed to be good. So I asked one of the Chinese girls about it. I asked her, 'Is this what Chinese food tastes like in China?' She looked at me, very surprised, and said, 'Is this supposed to be Chinese food?'

GUITARIST: Ha. You know what I miss? Halal-el-mashakel.

DRUMMER: I love halal-el-mashakel. [*A beat.*] Roasted chick peas…

GUITARIST: Yum. Pistachios…

DRUMMER: Mmm. Dried berries, sweets…

GUITARIST: Halal-el-mashakel. 'Problem solvers'. A bowl of Halal-el-mashakel and sweet tea—

DRUMMER: Or something stronger.

GUITARIST: And you can solve all the problems of the world.

   Pause.

DRUMMER: Have you seen the new girl? The Albanian? Lina?

GUITARIST: She's beautiful. Have you spoken with her? She's nice, too.

DRUMMER: I saw her first.

GUITARIST: You've got a girlfriend.

DRUMMER: Yeah.

GUITARIST: I thought you loved her.

DRUMMER: I do.

GUITARIST: So what are you doing looking at the new girl?

DRUMMER: My girlfriend was released. You know that. She lives in Adelaide with her family. I'm never going there, am I? And she's certainly not coming back to this hellhole.

   Pause.

GUITARIST: I was so young when we left. I've never had a girlfriend.

DRUMMER: Yeah, well, you'll probably never get one either.

   GUITARIST *looks away and starts strumming but is too upset to sing.* DRUMMER *stands up, walks to window. A beat.*

Ever think of escaping?

GUITARIST: Why do you think I was beat up?

DRUMMER: I thought—

GUITARIST: You thought wrong. I don't talk about it much.

DRUMMER: I'm… surprised.

GUITARIST: Didn't get too far.

   A beat.

DRUMMER: I'd get far. [*Shoots out hand like rocket*] That'd be me. Outta here.

GUITARIST: When anger gets you going, you still don't know where you're going. And even if you get there—

DRUMMER: You get somewhere.

GUITARIST: Maybe that's not where you want to be.

DRUMMER: Anywhere is better than here.

GUITARIST: I wouldn't know. They caught me before I could find out.

> DRUMMER *goes back to drum kit. Bangs on it for a moment while* GUITARIST *watches. Puts down sticks.*

DRUMMER: Fuck this.

> DRUMMER *takes another cigarette, lights up, offers one to* GUITARIST, *who shakes his head.* DRUMMER *starts to pace.*

GUITARIST: Why don't we try playing together again?

DRUMMER: What's the point?

GUITARIST: Music is its own point.

DRUMMER: I suppose. Kills time.

GUITARIST: No. Just the opposite. Music builds something out of time. Even the Jews in the concentration camps played music.

DRUMMER: Terrific. And then what happened to them?

GUITARIST: That's not the point.

GUARD: [*off stage*] Sa'id Ihram, report to immigration. Sa'id Ihram.

> GUITARIST *jumps to his feet, drops guitar.* DRUMMER *jumps to his. They embrace.*

DRUMMER: Good luck.

> GUITARIST *exits.* DRUMMER *returns to drum kit. Puts his face in his hands.*

SCENE TWO

DRUMMER *executes a slow drum roll.* GUITARIST *returns. Walks over to stool, sits down. Drum roll stops. Pause.*

GUITARIST: No. Don't say a thing.

> DRUMMER *holds out hand. Does a thumbs up, thumbs down. No reaction from* GUITARIST. *A beat.*

I ran into Mustafa. Today's soccer match between Stage Two and Three is cancelled. Their captain just been deported. It'll be rescheduled for a few days from now. When they find a new captain.

DRUMMER: They will. There's always new talent coming in.

> GUITARIST *stares straight ahead.* DRUMMER *waves to get his attention.* GUITARIST *ignores him.*

GUITARIST: Picks you up, slams you down.

DRUMMER: What's that?

GUITARIST: Hope.

> *Pause.* DRUMMER *studies* GUITARIST.

DRUMMER: [*picking up sticks*] Let's play something.

> *He starts 'Moonshadow'.*

GUITARIST: I'll play alright. They want to play with me, I'll play with them.

> GUITARIST *storms out of room. Sound of another door opening and slamming shut again offstage.* DRUMMER *plays a tattoo on the drum while this is happening.*

> GUITARIST *storms back in with a bottle in his hand. Wrenches off top, drinks it, falls on floor.* DRUMMER *rushes over, bends down, touches* GUITARIST's *face, checks label on bottle, throws it back onto the ground, jumps up and runs to the door.*

DRUMMER: Officer! Officer! Officer!

> *Sound of someone running towards the room.* GUARD *bursts in.*

GUARD: What's going on? [*Pointing to* GUITARIST] What happened? [*He spots the empty bottle.*] Bloody hell. Here, give me a hand, will ya?

> GUARD *and* DRUMMER *struggle to pick* GUITARIST *off the floor.* GUITARIST *is moaning. They exit, the* GUITARIST *supported by the other two.*

SCENE THREE

DRUMMER *and* GUITARIST *are sitting side by side on their stools.* DRUMMER *lights up a cigarette and offers one to the* GUITARIST, *who takes it, gets a light from the* DRUMMER *and inhales, coughing immediately. But he perseveres.*

DRUMMER: That was pretty fucking stupid.

> GUITARIST *shrugs.*

You said yourself if you stay sane, you win.

GUITARIST: They say we have one more appeal left.

DRUMMER: Appeal then.

GUITARIST: I suppose.

DRUMMER: You scared the shit out of me. What were you thinking?

> GUITARIST *shrugs. Pause.* DRUMMER *jumps off stool and paces.*

But shampoo? You can't kill yourself just by drinking shampoo. Fucking idiot.

GUITARIST: I suppose that was pretty stupid.

DRUMMER: What next? [*A beat.*] Conditioner?

GUITARIST: I thought maybe gel.

> DRUMMER *picks up a drum stick. Whacks* GUITARIST. GUITARIST *grabs stick, whacks him back. They start to laugh. The sound of the* GUARD's *voice brings the horsing around to a quick stop.*

GUARD: [*off stage*] Khalil Mubarak, please report to immigration. Khalil Mubarak.

> *They embrace.* DRUMMER *rushes out.* GUITARIST *picks up his instrument and picks out a song. He keeps looking up at the door. Finally,* DRUMMER *returns.*

DRUMMER: They're releasing me tomorrow.

> GUITARIST *embraces him.*

I'm... sorry. I wish it were both of us.

> GUITARIST *looks away, towards the window. After a moment, turns back to face* DRUMMER.

That's okay. It still might be. There's always that appeal.

DRUMMER: I… I'll be right back.

He exits, then returns with big plastic bag full of nuts and other small treats.

My stash. Halal-el-mashakel. Problem solvers. I'm sorry I didn't share any with you before.

He holds out the bag.

GUITARIST: [*taking a handful*] Halal-el-mashakel. What d'ya know.
DRUMMER: Take the whole bag.

He hands it over.

GUITARIST: Thanks. [*He puts the bag down.*] Wanna play a song?
DRUMMER: Whatever you like.

DRUMMER *gathers sticks. Sits down at drum kit.*

They start to play 'Moonshadow'. Very harmoniously.

GUARD: [*off*] Muster!

They put down their instruments, and go to the door.

Curtain.

THE END

Journey of Asylum –
Waiting

CATHERINE SIMMONDS
AND ASYLUM SEEKERS AND REFUGEES FROM
THE ASYLUM SEEKER RESOURCE CENTRE,
MELBOURNE

2010 Asylum Seeker Resource Centre production of Journey of Asylum – Waiting *in the Bella Union Theatre, Melbourne. (Photo: Riza Manalo.)*

Introduction

The Asylum Seeker Resource Centre (ASRC) was founded in 2001 by Konstandinos Karapanagiotidis. Based in Melbourne's inner-west, it is one of Australia's leading non-governmental asylum seeker advocacy, aid and health organisations. It also supports creative work, as *Journey of Asylum – Waiting* attests. One of two collaboratively written texts in this collection (the other being *CMI*), *Journey of Asylum* represents a collage of stories and personal histories, some of which bear their origins in testimony, while others are more poetic or symbolic. Narratives are often presented in parallel in such a way that time, place, history and imagination are unmoored and interwoven. Director-facilitator Catherine Simmonds worked with asylum seekers and refugees as well as Australian theatre makers and community workers; while the core objective of the project was the theatre piece that was staged at Bella Union in Melbourne in 2010, *Journey of Asylum – Waiting* was as much about *processes*—of creativity, skills development, confidence, friendship and community—as it was about the theatrical product.

The large cast of characters is divided into asylum seeker and refugee 'protagonists' and non-refugee 'collaborators'. The text exhibits clearly its genesis as a devised work responsive to the backgrounds and characteristics of its participants. All of the Australian characters' names and some of the asylum seekers' (with the exception of those who did not wish to publicise their identities in this book) are the performers' real names. This creates for the reader a constant sense of slippage, where a named individual behaves in various ways, taking on a number of 'characters' whilst still remaining in some essential way *themselves*. These slippages between actors and roles has the effect of highlighting the lenses though which interactions between asylum seekers and those from whom they seek assistance or protection are filtered: commercial (for the people smuggler characters), bureaucratic (for government and legal representatives), disinterestedly polite (for cabin crew), pedagogic (for teachers) and so on. The question then becomes, who exactly is interacting with whom—are we dealing with individuals or their socially constituted roles?

In *Refugees, Theatre and Crisis: Performing Global Identities* (2012), Alison Jeffers presents the compelling argument that asylum seekers who cross international borders become enmeshed in bureaucratic performances of 'refugeeness', being 'forced to play the role of "Convention refugees"' (p. 17) (she is referring here to the UN Refugee Convention), in the process becoming *conventional* in the sense of conforming to expectations of the powerless and persecuted. Bureaucratic performances of identity inflect theatre made by and about refugees for the purposes of social mobilisation, underpinning common narrative devices and the meanings that they communicate.

Journey of Asylum riffs on this issue of the roles individuals are made to play in different circumstances, especially across power differentials. It portrays legalistic interactions that frame 'conventional' refugeeness, but it also stages resistance. In doing so, it implicates the audience/reader, provoking us to evaluate our own desire to hear the refugees' traumatic stories in the first place. In the play's second vignette, asylum seeker Haydar expresses a deep weariness: 'I'm sick of telling my story; talk talk talk talk talk. I already told my story. It doesn't work'. What Haydar is saying here is something Jeffers recognises: that adhering to bureaucratic performance codes often brings little hope of formalised refugee status. At the start of the next vignette, asylum seeker Yomal, lying seductively in a Perspex box, teases the audience: 'Give me a banana and I will tell you a story. Give me two bananas and I'll tell you my story, but maybe you won't sleep for the rest of your life'. The words ask us to think about what an individual might be reduced to in the face of demands to tell and retell their 'story'. The words also, subversively, present the prospect that stories may be tailored to satisfy spectatorial appetites.

Uniquely among the plays in this book, *Journey of Asylum* portrays experiences—some humourous, others agonising, still others prosaic—of resettlement. In one scene, the process of reorienting oneself to a new home draws from African refugees' memories of culture shock upon first encountering Melbourne's busy Flinders Street Station. In this scene, as elsewhere in the play, the shock is distilled in physical theatre techniques that show just how intimately culture is written on the body.

Cumulatively, the vignettes that make up *Journey of Asylum* (and on a meta level, the collective context in which the work took shape) build a picture of how countless human interactions, big and small, personal and impersonal, crucially determine the course of asylum seekers' lives. If asylum seekers are the 'protagonists' here, citizens must, as *Journey of Asylum* signals, become 'collaborators', with all of the ambiguity that word implies. Or as Jeffers puts it, 'there can be no hospitality without risk. That risk is taken on both sides because, in the truly hospitable encounter, both host and guest must be prepared to be changed' (p. 162).

Emma Cox

Journey of Asylum – Waiting was first produced by the Asylum Seeker Resource Centre, Melbourne, at the Bella Union Theatre, Melbourne's Trades Hall, on 16 March 2010, under the following creative leadership:

Director, Catherine Simmonds
Arts Project Manager, Heidi Abdel-Raouf

Many of the asylum seekers and refugees who performed in *Journey of Asylum – Waiting* do not wish to expose their identities. For the purposes of consistency, none of the actors' names are provided here.

A NOTE ON THE TEXT

This script was created through a process of workshops, meetings, dialogues, improvisations and rehearsals with asylum seeker and refugee participants. The *mise-en-scene* often comprises multiple and parallel realities. Characters at times simultaneously play themselves and the characters of their memories. The written English is not always grammatically correct as it reflects the spoken English of many of the characters. Stage directions indicate when a character is speaking in a language other than English, but the written text remains entirely in English. The large number of characters and the specific languages used reflects the composition of participants in the ASRC's production.

CHARACTERS

Asylum seeker and refugee characters (the PROTAGONISTS):

ZAID	VIENNA	MICK
YOMAL	ANGEL	ANDY
HADIJA	TENGENE	LIONEL
TESAFAY	AHMAN	ALI
UBAX	ANBESSA	AMANI
TSEWANG	ASLAM	ISMAN
NADIA	HAYDAR	OMAR

Australian characters (the COLLABORATORS):

TRIBUNAL MAN	MEMBER	DAN
SARAH	TANIA	CLARE
NIKKI	MERRYN	SIMON
DOROTHY	HEIDI	FEDERAL POLICE OFFICER
IMMIGRATION OFFICER		

DESIGN AND SETTING

A large projection screen is attached to exposed scaffolding. Multimedia footage is projected onto the screen throughout the performance. The projector is also linked to a hand-held 'surveillance' camera. A ladder attached to the scaffolding leads to a platform containing an archive of case files. Ten clear portable Perspex screens (six foot tall on wheels; some with small windows) are used to define spaces and places; the actors also write on them using marker pens. A large Perspex box contains a microphone and can be lit from within. The MEMBER sits on a high podium chair at the back of the audience and interjects from here throughout the performance.

Soundscapes are created with radio and television sound bites taken from interviews with politicians, reporters, as well as advertisements and television shows. Some soundscapes are also composed from interviews with other asylum seekers.

PROLOGUE

TRIBUNAL MAN *enters.*

TRIBUNAL MAN: [*addressing the audience*] Before we proceed, I must ask you to switch off your mobile phones and to state who you are and your relationship to the applicant. And I must inform you that the proceedings are being recorded. A Refugee Review Tribunal is independent of Immigration and it is therefore closed to the public.

Waits for the audience to answer before continuing.

Is there anyone else to be coming in? Okay, good. [*He closes a small window in one of the Perspex screens.*] Presiding over the cases is Member George Hamilton. As part of the formal proceedings I'll ask you all to stand when the Member enters the room. The hearing is to determine if our applicant is a refugee, according to the UN Convention. A refugee is a person who has fear; the Convention also says that there should be well-founded reasons for that fear. What a refugee fears is that they will be persecuted. Persecution is a serious form of harm or punishment. Not all reasons make a person a refugee. There are five possible reasons: Race. Religion. Nationality. Membership of a particular social group. Political opinion. Do you have any questions about what I have said so far? [*He asks the question but does not give the audience a chance to answer.*] The Member is now entering the room. Please stand.

MEMBER *enters and takes his seat on the high podium chair at the back of the audience.*

The Member has entered the tribunal room; the tribunal is now in session. [*He looks at the time.*] Commencing at 8.35 pm [*Or the actual time of the performance*].

TRIBUNAL MAN *exits.*

Soundscape: gusts of wind.

HADIJA *enters.*

VIENNA *enters carrying a clay bowl.*

143

AHMAN *enters and lies on the ground in a spot of light.*

TENGENE *enters carrying water in a metal bucket.*

SCENE ONE: I DON'T BELIEVE YOU

Continuation of previous scene.

TENGENE *gently holds* AHMAN *in his arms and washes his chest.*

VIENNA *slowly and ritualistically raises and tilts the clay pot, tipping blood upon her head.*

MEMBER: [*interrupting the action from the high podium*] I don't believe you.

VIENNA, TENGENE, AHMAN *and* HADIJA *exit.*

A closely huddled group of asylum seeker and refugee PROTAGONISTS *enters upstage. They move in unison toward the audience, exhibiting the following gestures:*

- *Tense arms and clenched fists that only release with a deep breath.*

- *Head down holding stomach with a sense of longing and sadness.*

- *Arms around throat as though attempting to strangle the self—the breath is laboured.*

- *Stomping action and a beating of the fist to the chest; the fist then becomes an accusatory pointed finger.*

- *Very slowly leaning backwards and placing hand over mouth in a gesture of silence.*

- *Rapid movement of feet, like thunder or a stampede as the performers move downstage.*

PROTAGONISTS *thrust* HAYDAR *forward and he falls to the floor. All except* HAYDAR *and* MEMBER *disperse and exit.*

SCENE TWO: THIS IS NOT AN ACT

HAYDAR: [*to the audience*] I'm sick of telling my story; talk talk talk talk talk. I already told my story. It doesn't work. I don't want to. Don't make me do this. Sorry, I don't want to play.

Refusing to perform, HAYDAR *moves to exit the stage but at the last moment turns to confront the audience.*

If I tell you my story, am I going to get PR: Permanent Residency? Am I? I already told Immigration, Refugee Review Tribunal; they took two years. I sent it to the Federal Court and I'm still waiting. All my documents are there. Why am I waiting? No work rights, no study rights, what for, to lose my brain? Who here has got their PR, put your hands up? You can tell your story if you've got permanent residency. I don't have PR. You can talk, you're free, you can say whatever you want, but I can't.

Who are you, the Government, Immigration, a spy of the Minister, who? A spy from my country, who? If I say one wrong thing about the Government, the rules, about the Minister, about anything in Australia, they'll kick me out. Without PR they can play me like a ball, kick me here, here, here. But if you have PR you have power.

Look I'm not actor, all right? It's my life. In the movies when you get shot, you stand up and do the scene again. This is my life. This is not an act.

HAYDAR *exits.*

SCENE THREE: GIVE ME A BANANA

Soundscape: [looped] 'The gold class seat is the ultimate in armchair comfort to put you in the perfect position to experience the movie, perfect position to experience the movie, perfect position to experience the movie'.

A light comes up within the Perspex box. YOMAL *is lying inside, in a seductive pose; he beckons intimately to the audience.*

YOMAL: Give me a banana and I will tell you a story. Give me two bananas and I'll tell you my story, but maybe you won't sleep for the rest of your life.

Black out.

ASLAM *appears, standing in a spotlight.*

DOROTHY *and* SARAH *are sitting in a row of chairs stage left. The following are parallel scenes.*

ASLAM: My name is Aslam Abawi. I arrived in Melbourne in the year 2000 seeking asylum.

DOROTHY: Where are you up to in the training course?

SARAH: Well, I've started visiting the Maribyrnong detention centre.

DOROTHY: That's brave of you.

ASLAM: I was granted a bridging visa until 9/11. After September eleven—

SARAH: What's brave about it?

DOROTHY: You don't expect to get attacked?

ASLAM: I was told to reapply to the Minister for a Humanitarian Visa. To cut a long story short, I was handed over to what is now known as the Department of Immigration and Citizenship.

SARAH: Attacked by whom?

DOROTHY: Those people who are locked up—

SARAH: I'm much more afraid of the guards.

IMMGRATION OFFICER *enters.*

IMMIGRATION OFFICER: Mr Abawi, you're under arrest.

ASLAM: What for?

IMMIGRATION OFFICER: Don't worry. It's not Guantanamo.

ASLAM: He called me a filthy camel and then said—

IMMIGRATION OFFICER: Just put on his file 'unidentified Afghan'.

All exit except MEMBER.

SCENE FOUR: BORDER CONTROL

Soundscape: airport arrival and departure calls.

IMMGRATION OFFICER *enters and sits at a counter.* CLARE *enters, with a megaphone.*

CLARE: Would all passengers on flight E457 please make your way to gate lounge number twenty-two.

> PROTAGONISTS *and* MERRYN *enter, forming a long queue stage left, facing the audience.* MERRYN, *an Australian returning from a holiday in Bali, is at the front of the queue; she intermittently waves enthusiastically to the audience, as though they are friends who she can see through the doors to the waiting area.*

IMMIGRATION OFFICER: [*opening a window in a Perspex screen*] Next.

> MERRYN *goes to the counter and quickly clears customs. Exits.*

Next.

> TENGENE *walks to the counter.*

> IMMGRATION OFFICER *takes a long, deliberate stare at* TENGENE; *examines his passport then looks back again at him. This sequence is repeated a few times.* TENGENE *nervously turns to look at the person in the queue behind him. In a domino affect, people turn to look at the person behind and thus deflect the implication that they themselves may be the subjects of suspicion.*

SCENE FIVE: BORDERS, BAG SEARCH, CUSTOMS, BORDERS

Continuation of previous scene.

Soundscape: [looped; continues throughout the scene] 'Intercepted another boat. Were on board a boat intercepted. Were intercepted. Intercepted the people on that boat. Here illegally. Illegal immigration'.

TSEWANG *and* LIONEL *have been chosen. They leave the queue and follow the* IMMGRATION OFFICER *to a table.*

PROTAGONISTS *turn away, hiding their faces with their hands.*

IMMIGRATION OFFICER *stands staring out at the audience.* TSEWANG *is upset at having been singled out. He removes things from his backpack.* LIONEL *slowly removes his shoes and watch.*

OMAR, *from within the* PROTAGONISTS' *queue, begins to vomit.*

Stage lights turn upon the audience, immersing them in bright light. SARAH, NIKKI *and* SIMON *enter and accost the audience, checking bags, tickets, forms of identification, etc.*

SARAH: [*taking an audience* MEMBER'*s bag and threatening to empty the contents of the bag*] Have you anything to declare? I have to inspect the contents of your bag.

SIMON: [*to audience*] You're lucky it's just a play.

UBAX: [*from within the* PROTAGONISTS' *queue*] My story, that's all I've got, that's all I came with.

IMMIGRATION OFFICER: Your visa has been cancelled. You have to leave the country in the next forty-eight hours.

SCENE SIX: DISORIENTED—THE LIFT

Continuation of previous scene.

Soundscape: [looped; words layered upon sounds of counter bells and lift doors] 'level eleven, going down; counter three; level one, going up; ticket number three; level eight, going down...'

LIONEL, *from within the* PROTAGONISTS' *queue, wanders in a disoriented state.* PROTAGONISTS *are buffeted around like leaves in the wind.*

COLLABORATORS *enter. Rhythmically, the* COLLABORATORS *turn the screens, conjuring the revolving doors of relentless bureaucracy.*

HADIJA: [*dazed and confused; whispering into a microphone*] Just looking; I can't hear anything. What's my name, who are they calling? Is it me they are calling, was it me?

Soundscape: [looped; words layered over the sound of a plane engine] 'ticket number one, level one, level eight, going down, level ten, going up, level fifteen...'

PROTAGONISTS *cluster as though waiting for a lift. Upon the sound of lift doors opening, they step into a square of light and look upward.* YOMAL *climbs the ladder.*

YOMAL: Have you seen that movie *Shine*, with Geoffrey Rush? Remember when he says, 'Everyone else is going up and I'm going down?'

He descends the ladder.

PROTAGONISTS *spill out from the lift. All exit except* MEMBER.

SCENE SEVEN: IMMIGRATION

CLARE, ANGEL *and* YOMAL *enter.*

ANGEL: [*on the phone to her brother in Rwanda*] Hey brother, this is Angel... Of course I'm good, this is Aussie, half heaven, lucky country. Anyway, tomorrow I am going to the tribunal... Relax, I didn't rob the bank, or sell drugs. This is the Aussie tribunal, different to Rwandan tribunal. Don't worry; it's just a process to get my visa. Just pray for me. When I win you will win too.

Soundscape: 'ticket number one, counter one; ticket number two, counter two...'

YOMAL *sits on a stool. Perspex screens are placed around him to create a booth.*

PROTAGONISTS *enter and sit stage left on a long line of stools.* PROTAGONISTS *move in a choreographed sequence of actions that express their restlessness during the long wait. Extremely slowly,* LIONEL *removes all his clothes and folds them until he remains in his underpants. He crawls into the Perspex box and curls into a foetal position.*

CLARE: [*standing outside the booth behind* YOMAL, *she opens a small window and conducts the session*] The phone number you gave, is it correct?

YOMAL: Yes.

CLARE: Are you sure, cause I just tried.

She shows him a piece of paper with a number written on it.

YOMAL: [*regarding the paper*] Oh, no, that's my old number.

CLARE: Oh, then what's your new number?

YOMAL: It's on my other forms and my lawyer has this… I get confused sometimes.

CLARE: [*sceptically*] Okay, so what's your new number?

YOMAL *writes his new number on* CLARE'*s piece of paper.*

I just tried calling, why is it not calling?

YOMAL: My phone is on silent.

CLARE: When my phone is on silent it vibrates! Look, your case is very complex and I am assigned here to handle it in a professional manner. As you are aware, your case has been to the Minister and you are now here on departure grounds.

YOMAL *is in a state of shock.*

ASLAM: [*standing up from his stool*] Deportation.

YOMAL: What, the Minister? What, I don't know anything, when, I… um, what…?

CLARE: We would have sent documents to your lawyer.

YOMAL: My lawyer never said that.

CLARE: Well, we did. That's very odd. One moment, I'll go and check the…

YOMAL *remains in booth.* CLARE *exits.*

SCENE EIGHT: DEPARTURE GROUNDS

Soundscape: immigration reception area; sounds of phone calls, conversations and the television.

MERRYN, NIKKI, SARAH *and* DAN *enter and stand behind the Perspex screens, facing the audience.*

LIONEL *remains curled in a foetal position in the Perspex box throughout the scene. The other* PROTAGONISTS *create four queues; their backs to the audience, they move in a choreographed sequence towards* MERRYN, NIKKI, SARAH *and* DAN. *The following dialogue overlaps to give the effect of simultaneous interviews.*

MERRYN: May I see your passport, please?—

NIKKI: I can see here you're on a Student Visa—

SARAH: I've got pictures here that show you actively protesting here in Melbourne; however, you never actively protested in China—

DAN: That's an interesting name. I need proof of identification—

MERRYN: I see you're here on departure grounds… are you aware of this?—

NIKKI: Why did it take you three years to apply for a protection visa?—

SARAH: It appears to me that you are protesting now merely to strengthen your case—

DAN: If you were so fearful of torture, why did it take you fourteen days to leave the country?—

NIKKI: It makes me doubtful that you're a refugee—

MERRYN: You need to leave Australia within fourteen days—

DAN: If you were a person of prominence, they would have detained you—

SARAH: We consider this to be an act of bad faith—

NIKKI: I will not be a victim to your emotional blackmail—

MERRYN: You are technically unlawful, so I need you to sign this bridging visa—

DAN: So now you're placing blame on your migration agent?—

NIKKI: Your visa was cancelled. You've been living here illegally for eight months—

DAN: The Department of Foreign Affairs and Trade does not indicate your country is unsafe—

MERRYN: Should you not comply, I'm afraid I will have to detain you—

SARAH: Do you understand how this looks to me?

> SIMON *enters, as an officer, and stands in a spotlight. He opens his big coat, exposing large pockets full of forms. The* MEMBER *and* SIMON *simultaneously question* NADIA.

SIMON: Have you come with evidence that you are making arrangements to depart Australia?

NADIA: I have a son in Sri Lanka; my mum, she's a widow. I need to study but they stopped paying for my study. I need to send my son money, he needs things, I can't go home, that's why I am here.

MEMBER *and* SIMON: What's more important: your study or your son?

NADIA: My study is for my son, but I can't study.

SIMON: How old is your son?

NADIA: Eight years old.

SIMON: How long since you've seen him?

NADIA: Four years.

MEMBER *and* SIMON: A son needs a mother doesn't he? If you love your son and your mother you would go back, wouldn't you?

NADIA: Go back and ruin his life, his future? No, I need to stay and study, to get a life and say 'fuck you' to all my relations and that narrow minded society who humiliate me. My son's life depends on my success and me. I don't want to poison us again as I did in the past.

MEMBER: Your evidence doesn't really amount to fear of persecution.

NADIA: Well you can't understand, I don't blame you, you're an Australian not a Sri Lankan, and you're a man.

SIMON: I can give you a Sri Lankan officer.

NADIA: And how will they treat a single Mum?

SIMON: You said you would go to the Sri Lankan Embassy to get a passport. You said you would supply a plane ticket. I need to be satisfied that you are making genuine arrangements to depart Australia.

All exit except LIONEL *and* MEMBER.

SCENE NINE: WE'RE ALL HUMAN

CLARE *and* YOMAL *enter.* CLARE, *as* IMMGRATION OFFICER, *resumes session with* YOMAL.

CLARE: For some reason, I had thought you were on departure grounds, but you're not. Can you just sign here to verify the mistake?

YOMAL *signs the paper.*

A small mistake, we're all human.

CLARE *and* YOMAL *exit.*

SCENE TEN: LONELY—LIKE A RED LIGHT OUT TO SEA

LIONEL *is still curled in a foetal position in the Perspex box, which is lit from within.*

LIONEL: There were five of them; they seemed like they'd come to kill me; at first I thought it was a joke, until I slept the night and I realised I was in detention, like a dead person; it's an unbelievable state, like a dream... my mind was gone, I didn't know where it was.

Soundscape: wind, water and the bell of a boat at sea.

The stage is dark, apart from the Perspex box. PROTAGONISTS *enter and move slowly about the space, dancing with red bike lights, which flash in the dark. The image conjures a lonely ship at night.*

Soundscape: [looped] 'immigration, no man's land, take them to Christmas Island and detain them there. Christmas Island detention centre can hold 1400 people. The growing numbers. Boosted to accommodate an influx of boat people. Stay for a certain period of time. The crowded Christmas Island detention centre. Despite the growing numbers of detainees. A Sri Lankan girl. Refugees. Children detained. Detainees. Detainees. Detained. Being detained in. The detention centre in... Detention facility. Detention camps. Deportation deportation deportation deportation deportation deportation...'

LIONEL *remains in a foetal position. The* PROTAGONISTS, *carrying red bike lights, climb onto the Perspex box. It looks like a Christmas tree flashing in the dark. These are the people crowded in boats or detention centres.* LIONEL *peeks out from the box. On the word in soundscape, 'deportation', all exit except* LIONEL *and* MEMBER.

MEMBER: So what are you gonna do now?

LIONEL: I don't know but I can't go back to Zimbabwe.

MEMBER: This is the list of visas you can apply for. [*He holds up a document.*] The system has cancelled your student visa your only real option is a protection visa.

LIONEL: Can I apply for a skilled visa?

MEMBER: You don't have the qualifications.

LIONEL: Okay. I'll apply for protection.

MEMBER: We'll start the application process but you'll remain in detention.

Black out. LIONEL *exits, unseen.*

SCENE ELEVEN: BODY SEARCH

AMANI, UBAX, TANIA *and* NIKKI *enter.*

AMANI *and* UBAX *stand behind two separate screens; the stage lights are low. They stand with their legs apart and slowly raise their arms in unison. Simultaneously* TANIA *and* NIKKI, *as* IMMGRATION OFFICERS, *ritualistically and slowly trace their bodies with red lights.* AMANI *and* UBAX *move in unison in a strange dance as the red lights search and trace their bodies.*

Soundscape: [an electronic scanner sound is layered with voice] 'I'm thinking about the airport and immigration, what will we do, we'll go to jail? And still my son is young and I am running the fighting my country. This is no good, but even no good is risky. When I come Australia in the night-time, all the light, I said, oh beautiful the country, but I am scared, cause the airport stay, the immigration. My son is cry, I afraid, I afraid, only the people of the country and airport and the passport and the visa, I am scared, a lot of scared because I'm not my passport, not my name, not my passport, even not my face, another face, that why I'm scared, I am scared, I go to jail, I feel like that I don't know where we go even and I don't have the bag, me and my son no bag anything'.

All exit except MEMBER.

SCENE TWELVE: WHY DIDN'T YOU SAY YOU WERE A REFUGEE?

ZAID *enters and cautiously approaches the audience. Suddenly, he throws his bag to the ground, throws his hands in the air and drops to his knees.*

ZAID: I am a refugee from Iraq, I want the police... Arabic, Arabic, please sorry me no English, no English, Arabic, Arabic, no English, Arabic.

> VIENNA *enters.*

VIENNA: I speak Arabic.

> ZAID *speaks in Arabic.*

[*Translating into English*] I got off the plane. I was scared. I went to the toilet. I waited there. Ripped up my passport threw it in the toilet. Waited for the plane to go, so they can't send me back. I came to customs, threw my bag and I screamed loud, 'I am an Iraqi refugee, I want the police'. Then the police came; there was a pretty policewoman, and I thought, 'wow if this is the police then no worries, I'll go with them'. [*Laughs*] Bloody typical Iraqi man. [*Continuing the translation*] But there were ten of them and she was the harshest of them all. They took me to one room with a camera for eight hours.

> ZAID *walks to the surveillance camera.* VIENNA *exits.*

MEMBER: If you lic you may go to prison for ten years.

ZAID: Better than going back to my country.

> *He exits.*

SCENE THIRTEEN: CAN'T GO HOME

Soundscape: Australian birds in the bush mixed with the sound of wings in a cage.

TESAFAY: [*entering through the audience*] Do you know where I can buy a calling card to call Africa?

ANBESSA *and* TENGENE *enter.*

ANGEL: [*entering with a megaphone, impersonating a phone company's automated message*] 'To recharge your card, press one. To speak to a customer service consultant, press three...'

She exits.

ANBESSA, TENGENE *and* TESAFAY *simultaneously speak on the phone to their families in their respective languages. Intermittently they switch to English.*

ANBESSA, TENGENE *and* TESAFAY: I can't come home.

ANBESSA: But you said.

TENGENE: Don't come back home.

ANBESSA, TENGENE *and* TESAFAY: Why, why?

ANBESSA: My friend is in jail because he sang that song I wrote.

TESAFAY: [*as his mother*] I begged you not to sing that song. You can't come back, my son. Two days after you left the police came and took your sister; they wanted her to tell them where you went. Your cousin is in jail. My son, don't call me, they might take me too. Don't call me again. Don't call me. God bless you, Amen.

ANBESSA: Every step I take I think of you—

TENGENE: I wake thinking, is my Mum all right—

ANBESSA: I imagine how my children are without my help—

TENGENE: I love her; I could not tell her what really happened—

ANBESSA: When you cannot speak life is zero. Just I wait...

ANBESSA, TENGENE *and* TESAFAY: I can't go back.

TESAFAY *sings.*

PROTAGONISTS *enter and stand in the dark with bike lights held like hearts to their chests. Two rapidly cross the stage, stabbing* TESAFAY *on both sides of his stomach.* TESAFAY *drops to the ground and crawls off the stage.*

CLARE: [*enters, speaking into a megaphone*] Ladies and gentlemen, we are about to enter some turbulence. Please remain calm and make sure you fasten your seat belts and that your tray tables are in an upright position.

Perspex screens become the walls of the immigration waiting room. PROTAGONISTS *enter the waiting area.* AHMAN, *carrying a pillow, lies down on top of the Perspex box.* TSEWANG *spins a prayer wheel. The theatre darkens and there is the effect of flashing light expressive of distant rocket fire.* AHMAN *tosses and turns. Other* PROTAGONISTS *sit; they too are disturbed and restless.* TSEWANG *spins the prayer wheel, reciting an incessant mantra.*

SCENE FOURTEEN: TERRORISTS/DICTATORS

Continuation of previous scene.

AHMAN *suddenly falls off the Perspex box. Waking from a nightmare, he goes to wash his face. He walks back to the box and climbs inside.*

Soundscape: muffled sound of AHMAN*'s family in daily life chatting around the dinner table, making jokes, etc.*

AHMAN: [*from within the box*] The moment I arrived here, till now, I don't behave like a normal person. I can't eat properly.

TANIA *enters.*

TANIA: Are you homesick?

AHMAN: Yes, I have a wonderful family. I miss them a lot.

ALI: [*to the audience*] Have you ever been in love?

TSEWANG: My dad was seventeen when he fell in love.

ALI *recites a love poem in Arabic.*

TSEWANG *stops his prayer wheel and moves to the action of riding and holding a big yak by the horns. He moves between the character of himself and his father. When he speaks as his father he speaks in Tibetan.*

TSEWANG: [*to audience*] He used to take the Yaks to graze in Lhasa. Have you heard of Lhasa? Do you know Tibet?

ALI: You know the River Nile—it flows from the heart of Africa.

TSEWANG: There were monasteries with prayer flags whispering in the wind. He used to watch mum coming down from monastery everyday to milk the yak.

ALI: [*describing the story with gestures of one hand*] How beautiful is the light of the River Nile. She was crying; it was the first time she had ever seen the River Nile. Sim, Sim, I will pluck the stars and make necklace for you. One day I will take you to the moon. And build you a house. I love you.

TSEWANG: [*kneeling in the position of marriage proposal*] He asked for her hand, her parents said, no, so he just got on a horse and rode. Until there she was, this beautiful woman and she jumped on the back of the horse and they just ran away and had five beautiful children and I am one of them. He said, 'Son you are Tibetan but you don't know the taste of Yak milk, you grew up in Nepal—you been drinking cows milk all your life'.

ALI: The government security forces ordered my lady into their car and me to follow them on their motorcycles. The leader said, 'We have a mobile photo that shows you were hugging and kissing this woman'. I said, I made no mistake, we are getting married, and we have rings on our fingers we are going to be married. An old woman once read my coffee cup. She told me, my son, your cup looks very sad for the future. Soldiers and dogs guard your girl, a long and difficult journey lies in front but you will get there.

AHMAN: [*from within the Perspex box*] I don't know where to start. I'll start with my Dad. He's a real hero, not a film hero. He was a friend to us and he's done so many honourable things in his life, always trying to teach us. I can never be like my father. I don't have such a big heart, and my mother was strong, mentally strong, encouraging us always.

He pauses as he feels the threat of what could happen.

MEMBER: State your country of birth.

OMAR: [*to the audience*] When I say Pakistan, I know what you think, go on, admit it. [*He lifts his shirt.*] You think I'm one of them.

ASLAM: [*sitting down and miming a typewriting action*] I am from Afghanistan, but spent many years in Pakistan.

He places a blindfold over his own eyes.

AHMAN: I'm Hazara, from Afghanistan, but spent my life in Pakistan, in a city called Quetta, close to the border of Afghanistan.

OMAR: Quetta, that's one of the worst places in Pakistan, a bad place for any human being.

AHMAN: The Americans call it the Taliban heaven. Have you been there?

OMAR: No.

AHMAN: The fundamentalists have a saying, if you kill one Hazara you'll go to heaven; if you kill two Hazaras, you and your family will go to heaven.

OMAR: I don't know who Hazaras are, to be very honest.

AHMAN: [*to the audience*] Have you seen the movie *The Kite Runner*? The little boy who was raped; he's Hazara.

OMAR *starts to slowly tie a blindfold around his own eyes.*

ASLAM *goes to his knees.*

MEMBER: So you claim to be a journalist, a journalist of some note, apparently?

ASLAM: I have a few documents, but that's all I took.

MEMBER: We know your country's corrupt. How do I know this is real?

ASLAM: They're real.

MEMBER: From what I can ascertain you sound like an everyday journalist, why would they be interested in you? The Taliban, the warlords, whoever you call them, you don't really know, do you, who exactly it is that is after you?

ASLAM: There are so many different groups who want to hurt you, they could be anyone.

MEMBER: Let me read from your statement. 'Men in white with long beards'. That could be anyone.

OMAR *goes to his knees.*

You do understand that the interview will be in English and that you need no translator and that it is a criminal offence if you say anything false. Do you have any questions?

OMAR: Can I ask you to repeat something if I don't understand? English is my second language.

MEMBER: But you chose not to have an interpreter.

OMAR: I was scared they might get what I say wrong.

MEMBER: Okay, Omar, I will do my best to accommodate you today. Can you tell me why you can't go home?

OMAR: I fear persecution from the terrorist organisation named in my statement.

MEMBER: Which organisation are you referring to?

OMAR: Haven't you read my statement? It's written there fifty times; they are the second biggest terrorist organisation in the world. Read the first page, paragraph two.

MEMBER: Calm down, Omar, there is no need for that tone. [*He reads again.*] I would like to start with the first time that you claim they came to your home. Tell me the date they came looking for you.

OMAR: I don't know the exact date; May or June, it is just an approximate date in my statement.

MEMBER: Tell me if there's anything else that's approximate in your statement? Dates that are incorrect, etc.

OMAR: One mistake can drag you into hell. Once you slip, you just keep slipping. I can't answer your questions.

Spotlight on AHMAN *in the Perspex box.* TANIA *enters and speaks simultaneously with* AHMAN *into a microphone.*

AHMAN *and* TANIA: What do you think of those warlords?

AHMAN: Ugly monster. I see a lot of them flashing in my eyes.

AHMAN *and* TANIA: What do you see flashing in your eyes?

AHMAN: Those faces. Those scenarios.

AHMAN *and* TANIA: Whose face?

AHMAN: Terrorist face.

AHMAN *and* TANIA: What do they look like?

AHMAN: Like a normal person but I recognise their hatred...

All exit except MEMBER.

SCENE FIFTEEN: FIGHT THE INSURGENTS

Soundscape: 'send an additional 30,000 US troops to Afghanistan... American forces in Iraq'. [followed by a looped repetition]: 'Insurgents, civilians, soldiers, insurgents, civilians, soldiers, insurgents, civilians, soldiers, insurgents, civilians, soldiers, insurgents, civilians, soldiers...'

ZAID *enters. He receives a mobile phone message. A friend of his has been killed in a bomb blast. He throws the mobile phone to the ground and goes to his knees. He laments in Arabic interspersed with a few English words.*

VIENNA *enters, singing in Arabic.*

ZAID *stands and dances; he wants to remember the good. He remembers the beauty of Baghdad. He speaks in Arabic of a place called Abu Nuwas and as he does he takes out a book of poetry.*

ANGEL, YOMAL *and* TESAFAY *enter. Each stands in front of a screen; their backs are to the audience as they draw trees, maps and landscapes of their respective countries.*

VIENNA: I know that place Abu Nuwas. It's a famous place in Baghdad next to the Tigris, beautiful restaurants with date palms that line the river, like Southbank here in Melbourne. They named Abu Nuwas after the poet Abu Nuwas; there was a statue of him drinking wine and writing with two women next to him. He was a romantic poet.

ZAID *recites a poem in Arabic by Abu Nuwas.*

[*Dancing a very slow belly dance whilst she translates the poem*] I knew you always loved me and that you wanted me. But now you are trying to avoid me. Time has changed you and time changes everything. If you think that leaving me is sane, then God has taken sanity from you.

ANGEL, YOMAL *and* TESAFAY *stop drawing.*

Now on the corners there are no restaurants, and no statue of the poet.

ZAID: I knew an Iraq when none of this mattered. My father was Sunni, my mother was Shiite, my neighbours were Christian, we all shared food. Now the world is a big jungle and the strong eat the weak.

TESAFAY: In Ethiopia, we have a saying: 'the Americans get sick of watching movies at home, so they come and make real life action movies in Africa'.

All exit except MEMBER.

SCENE SIXTEEN: EDUCATION

ANDY *and* TENGENE *enter.*

ANDY: [*draws maps on the Perspex screens as though teaching a class*] We have two types of deserts, natural deserts and man-made deserts. Men made deserts are expanding rapidly. If you see, the Equatorial Rainforests are destroyed, the Amazon River and the natural waterfalls are drying up, and the impact of this is, global warming, climate change, drought and starvation. Whose responsibility is this? The developed countries have the political, economic, and technological power to stop this. However, it is the responsibility of all nations and it is our responsibility too.

TENGENE: African governments are always interested in their police, power, military security, their investment in buying guns and war.

MEMBER: [*to* TENGENE] All you did was write a magazine for homeless people.

TENGENE: I tried to advocate to the international media.

MEMBER: [*to* ANDY] You're just a teacher.

ANDY: A teacher is someone who assists people to develop their thinking and to change their attitudes. Sometimes being a teacher is a risk.

MEMBER: [*to* TENGENE] Sounds like you're more of a social worker, not very controversial?

TENGENE: Authorities can turn up at midnight, beat people, burn their plastic houses, put them in jail, that's the way it is; that is the cost of freedom of speech. You grew up in a democracy, you don't understand.

All exit except MEMBER.

SCENE SEVENTEEN: HOMELESS GIRLS PLAY SOCCER

Soundscape: 'primary school, I remember that. Left hand, right hand, bullet rocket. Left hand, right hand, bullet rocket…' [The words speed up to become almost indistinguishable; this is layered over a background sound of machine gun fire.]

ANGEL *enters. She writes on a Perspex screen and chants in French.*

MICK, ISMAN *and* LIONEL *enter. They write mathematical equations on the screens.*

ANGEL: I was very good in French. I was top of my class in geography chemistry, mathematics too. Paul bought 10 kilos of rice; someone steal him 3 kilos; so how much Paul got now?

MICK: Thirteen—

LIONEL: Four—

ISMAN: Five—

ANGEL: I said, me teacher, me! Seven.

> MICK, ISMAN *and* LIONEL *run suddenly and shield themselves with the screens. They beckon* ANGEL *to hide. After a moment, she emerges from behind a screen.*

The principal came to check fee payments, who'd paid and who hadn't paid, and she found me. [*She enacts teacher.*] 'You don't want to pay?' [*She enacts her own answer.*] No money, just wait, tomorrow I will pay'. Tomorrow was tomorrow; I couldn't say no money, cause no money means no going to school.

> ANGEL *grabs a ball and starts to play soccer with* MICK, ISMAN *and* LIONEL. *She outplays them and they exit.*

[*Monologue is punctuated by soccer moves*] I was famous on the streets. I was the only homeless girl to play soccer; most just use drugs. There was a coach who had a boy's team and he put me in his team. In my country we have interschool championships. If you can play for the school then you can go to school for free, so I should play hard, right? The cheapest public school is thirty thousand in Rwandan money, per semester. Imagine me, I don't have job, I don't have mother or father. I have my mum's sister. I used to call her 'little mum'. She can't help me cause she's poor, she has eight kids, she doesn't have husband, and she can't take me too. So I live with my two big brothers. Sometimes one brother gets money for food, but paying the rent is a problem and school fees, forget it.

So you see if I can't play, I can't study, I was playing for knowledge, that's why I say I played professional. Sometimes, I couldn't eat, my big brother said: 'Today no job, no money, so try to help yourself, okay'. Some of my stupid neighbours would say, 'Why you don't be a prostitute?', but I couldn't. If yesterday I went to my friend and asked for food, I can't go back again, it's embarrassing. So I just stay at home, practice my mathematics, my biology and forget about food, wake up, no breakfast go to school, walk one hour, study.

> ANGEL *calls* MICK, ISMAN and LIONEL, *who enter, arms around one another.*

I just stay with my poor friends and we share our poor. I used to encourage them, 'No worries man, future is there, god is one, we'll win this fucking life'.

> *She starts to train with* MICK, ISMAN *and* LIONEL *very intensively till she is out of breath.* MICK, ISMAN *and* LIONEL *exit.*

I have soccer training at three. I practice with hunger, no dinner, no breakfast, study, I do two hours practice, and then walk one hour home. If you get boiled beans, you eat boiled beans. We don't eat for healthy or not healthy, just to make your stomach full. 'Paul bought 10 kilos of rice; someone steal him 3 kilos; so how much Paul got now?'

> ANGEL *exits.*

SCENE EIGHTEEN: A NORMAL MORNING

UBAX *enters, carrying bags of groceries.*

UBAX: The group were forming to take over the whole of the country and as they were forming they were taking over one place after one place. They were taking schoolboys and putting them under their will, telling them they would die for God's sake. I was willing to fight but it's not like you could.

> SIMON *enters in a fluorescent life jacket, holding a surveillance camera.* UBAX's *face appears in projection.*

[*Speaking to the surveillance camera*] On a normal morning they blew the whole area, three or four shops in a row, when everybody was just going on with their daily life. They killed hundreds and hundreds of people in one blow. There was blood everywhere, body parts everywhere. My dad, brother were killed. I ran. My mum said, 'Go. Don't look back'. I stayed away, but I had to go back to know if my mum was still alive or not.

MEMBER: [*questioning* UBAX] If you were so afraid, why did you go back? That's not the actions of someone who fears for their life.

UBAX: I'd rather have died than leave her there alone.

MEMBER: Sounds like you just got caught up in a civil conflict. You weren't targeted individually.

UBAX: Everyone's dying.

MEMBER: So you accept you weren't targeted yourself.

UBAX: It's *war*!

    All exit except MEMBER.

SCENE NINETEEN: TORTURE

ZAID *enters. He sits on a stool, his hands above his head as though they are forcefully tied together. A Perspex booth is created around him.*

MEMBER: You asked for an interpreter.

    VIENNA *enters. She sits at a small window in one of the Perspex screens; she is transformed into the interpreter. She speaks in a very low voice into a microphone.*

You claim they hung you upside down.

    ZAID *speaks in Arabic.*

VIENNA: [*begins to translate into English but falters over some of the words; her mind will not let her utter them. As she speaks, the words are also projected*] They put me in the car; they took me to a deserted place. There were seven of them and they wanted money. I can make people laugh and smile but I can never forget waiting, thinking, how will they kill me? I have children. I didn't know what to do. A hook on the ceiling… they put my hands behind my back and hung me every day for fifteen days, asking what organisation I belonged to. I could hear people's voices in the other room. They were muffled. They brought a woman in—she used to work as a translator for the Americans—we spent days together... One day, maybe the fourteenth, they came. People came, put her hands behind her back; the man took his shoe and put it on her head then cut [*'her head' (in projection only)*] as if cutting a sheep. [*'Then they put her head in my lap' (in projection only)*]. I used to be a sportsman but I became weak. My family helped me to get to Turkey and I got sent back to Iraq. Now I am here; it is unbelievable that I am here. People in Australia are different, but beautiful.

All exit except MEMBER.

SCENE TWENTY: REFUGEE HOME AND AWAY

TENGENE, ANDY, LIONEL, ISMAN, ALI *and* ANGEL *enter and form a queue; they carry large plastic water cans and hessian sacks. Their backs are to the audience.*

MICK *enters and joins the queue; he is singing and holding hessian bags.*

MICK: Some days you can wait in a queue for a whole day, without getting anything. I used to get food and firewood from UNHCR every fifteen days. [*He opens his bags to receive his rations.*] One kilo of maize flour and 1 kilo of wheat flour, some oil, beans. [*He speaks directly to the audience.*] In the refugee camp we had only one video player and one film, so what I used to do is this...

He calls out in Dinka to AMANI, *who enters and takes his bag and gives him a coin. He calls* ALI *who takes his other bag in exchange for a coin.*

Get 20 Kenyan shillings, which is about 25 Australian cents, so I could go and watch.

ANDY, LIONEL, ISMAN *and* ANGEL *simultaneously run forward; they are fighting for a place to sit and watch the screen.*

[*He elbows and pushes his way to the front and he sits mesmerised and watch TV series,* Home and Away] WOW, it is very beautiful.

Soundscape: the theme song from Home and Away.

There is a silver car, the area is very green, there is even a little machine [*he imitates the lawn mower*] and beautiful type of food, not just beans and flour; look at what are they eating. Look at that pretty girl. I wish these things were in Africa. If I get settlement I will go to the *Home and Away* country. [*He stands.*] If I had the money to bribe a UNHCR official I would have been in Australia a long time ago, but I waited fourteen years in a refugee camp. [*He leaves and then turns back with an afterthought.*] Fourteen years, that's how it is for most people.

All exit except MEMBER.

SCENE TWENTY-ONE: SMUGGLER

UBAX *and* AMANI *enter. They perform the following as overlapping monologues, playing themselves and the people smugglers each encountered in Somalia.*

UBAX *washes a cloth in bucket of water. She stands, responding to the call of her aunt.*

AMANI: My name is Amani. I was told you could help me leave Somalia—

UBAX: [*as her aunt*] Yarat, this is Ubax. Ubax, this is Yarat. He'll be taking you—

UBAX: [*in Somali, as herself*] Where?

AMANI *in Somali, as a smuggler, asks for money.*

AMANI: Six thousand? I only have 390 dollars. Take this money from me, please, help me—

UBAX: [*in Somali, as herself*] Give me my money back—

UBAX: [*as her aunt*] Your Mum paid six thousand dollars to get you out; you're going with him. This is your passport.

AMANI: [*in Somali, as a smuggler*] Australia, Canada, America. Any of them I will take you—

UBAX: [*in Somali, as a smuggler*] Australia, Canada, America, Europe.

UBAX: [*as the aunt*] Listen, it's not safe here; you can't look after your mother. You have to go.

UBAX *is very upset. She retreats, she resists; she does not want to go.*

AMANI: I am scared to go prison, are you sure you can help me?

SCENE TWENTY-TWO: TAKE-OFF

Red bike lights are placed like a runway on the floor.

COLLABORATORS *enter as flight attendants to set the space for the plane.*

PROTAGONISTS *enter with stools and take their place on the plane.*

CLARE: Cabin crew: arm doors and cross check.

SIMON *and* TANIA *arrange the Perspex screens into a wall between the performers and the audience. They close the windows and stand ready for the safety demonstration. As she speaks, the actions of the* PROTAGONISTS *are choreographed like slapstick comedy. For most it is the first time they've ever been on a plane.*

Ladies and gentlemen, welcome on board flight AS653, direct to Melbourne. We are now preparing for take-off and although you may fly regularly, we would appreciate your full attention during our safety demonstration. Your seatbelt should be fastened low and tight across your lap. Should we experience a loss of cabin pressure, an oxygen mask will drop down in front of you. Simply secure the mask over your mouth and nose and oxygen will flow automatically. In the unlikely even of an emergency, strip lighting will illuminate your way to the exits.

Please note your nearest exit, remembering that it could be behind you. Exits are located at the front of the aircraft, at the rear, and over each wing. Please note that smoking on board the aircraft is a federal offence and bathrooms are fitted with smoke detectors. Ladies and gentlemen, thank you for choosing to fly with us today. Sit back, relax and enjoy your flight.

Cabin crew, prepare for take-off.

Passengers all lean back for a long time. ANGEL *and* UBAX *suddenly lurch forward and vomit.*

TANIA *and* SIMON: Chicken or Fish?

Soundscape: in-flight announcements.

ANGEL: Can I have both please? Some coconut…

MICK: Bool Bool?

TANIA *tries to communicate with* MICK.

[*Repeats*] Boool.

SIMON *and* TANIA: Sorry, we only have chicken and fish.

MICK*'s gestures are finally understood.* TANIA *points to the toilet. He runs to the back of the plane.*

SIMON: Oh, toilet.

ANGEL: Can I have some boiled beans, please?

CLARE: Cabin crew, prepare for landing. Well ladies and gentlemen, as you can see, we have made our descent into beautiful Melbourne. The local time is 6:04 pm and the temperature outside is a balmy 6 degrees. We hope you enjoyed your flight with us today; it's been a pleasure having you on board and we hope to have you back with us again soon. Now get your arses off my plane. Cabin crew, disarm doors and cross check.

All exit except MEMBER.

SCENE TWENTY-THREE:
FLINDERS STREET STATION—FIRST EXPERIENCES

PROTAGONISTS *enter and move around the space purposefully, as if at a busy station.*

AHMAN *starts to create a chalk drawing on the ground.*

ANGEL: [*imitating the train announcement through a megaphone*] Connex trains, departing from platform four… for Dandenong, Frankston and Craigieburn… remember to validate your Metcard before you travel.

TSEWANG: [*walks over to* AHMAN *and watches him draw*] Wow, that's beautiful.

TSEWANG, LIONEL *and* ASLAM *perform a hip-hop dance.*

All action freezes except for MICK *who weaves forward through the* PROTAGONISTS.

MICK: When I came to Australia 2006 I saw that life was different; different, not like *Home and Away.* When I first came to Flinders Street and I saw everybody rushing, rushing, busy people rushing and I feel afraid. Where are the people going, are the people migrating somewhere? I thought I was in a safe country. They say it is because people are busy rushing to the office, rushing for lunch. I became like somebody who didn't know what to do so I started imitating people, 'Hi, hi, hi, hi', but in Africa if you want to greet somebody you hug them. When I was in the refugee camp I used to go slow, slowly [*he imitates*], but in Australia...

He imitates a busy walk.

PROTAGONISTS *begin to rush about again, and then exit.*

There's a saying: 'when in Rome do what the Romans do'.

He exits.

SCENE TWENTY-FOUR: TAXI, RESTAURANT

TESAFAY, HAYDAR, TANIA, YOMAL *and* SARAH *enter. The following scenes are staged side by side. Each scene pauses as the other scene takes the focus.*

Taxi

TESAFAY: Okay, jump in. Where you going to?
TANIA: Hey, um, Williamstown.
HAYDAR: [*repeating*] Williamstown.
TESAFAY: Williamstown, no worries. [*To himself*] The meter is on. [*To* TANIA] Had a good night?
TANIA *and* HAYDAR: Yeah.

TESAFAY *checks the mirror.*

TANIA: Ah, so where are you from?

TESAFAY: I'm from Ethiopia.

TANIA: Oh, yeah.

TESAFAY: [*to the audience*] I been asked this question every night since I started driving taxis.

>   *Pause.*

Restaurant

YOMAL *and* SARAH *are seated. They both look at the menu.*

YOMAL: So what would you like to eat?

SARAH: I'm really hungry. You hungry?

YOMAL: Ah, not much.

SARAH: I really feel like some seafood. Have you ever had the lobster?

YOMAL: Yeah, yeah—

SARAH: Do you feel like drinking?

YOMAL: Yeah, I'll have a coke, please.

SARAH: I'll have a glass of Moet and the lobster as well, thank you.

>   NIKKI *enters, as waitress.*

NIKKI: What are you gonna have?

YOMAL: Um, I'm not that hungry.

NIKKI: Maybe some salad?

YOMAL: Yeah, I'll just have a garden salad.

NIKKI: Have you tried it before?

YOMAL: Yeah, yeah, oh… yeah.

>   NIKKI *exits.*

SARAH: So have you been on a date with an Australian woman before?

YOMAL: No this is my first time…

>   *Pause.*

Taxi

TANIA: They have a drought there, right?

TESAFAY: Sorry?

TANIA: In Ethiopia, a famine, no a drought, I mean a famine, no it was a drought... ah, poverty.

TESAFAY: Of course, there's poverty; but it's mostly man-made. We don't have natural disasters, no tsunami or earthquake; it's from man made problems: civil war, dictators in power—

TANIA: Corruption, yeah corruption.

TESAFAY: You guys are lucky to be Australian. I don't know how much you realise it but...

HAYDAR: [*touching* TESAFAY*'s dreadlocks*] Is that natural hair or...?

TESAFAY: Excuse me, please, I'm driving.

> HAYDAR *yawns and puts his feet up.*

Excuse me...

> *Pause.*

Restaurant

SARAH: [*drinks and devours food*] Sure you don't want some?

YOMAL: No, no, I'm fine.

SARAH: So the movie might start soon; shall we get the bill?

> NIKKI *enters.*

Can we please have the bill?

YOMAL: Yeah, so a movie, yeah.

> *The bill arrives and there is an awkward moment as* SARAH *looks away, expecting him to pay.*

Do, do you wanna give me a second? I need to go to the bathroom.

> *He runs away, smiling at the audience as he runs.*

> *Pause.*

Taxi

TANIA: Ah, excuse me, where are we?

TESAFAY: We are in Williamstown now.

TANIA: No, no, we said Thomastown.

HAYDAR: [*echoes*] Thomastown.

TESAFAY: Excuse me?

TANIA *and* HAYDAR: Thomastown.

TESAFAY: You said Williamstown.

TANIA: No, no. English is your second language. No, we're not paying.

Pause.

Restaurant

NIKKI: [*as waitress*] That bill ready?

SARAH: He'll be back soon.

All exit except MEMBER.

SCENE TWENTY-FIVE: MISSED CALLS, ALONE WITH THE TV

AMANI *enters. She looks at her phone; she has missed calls.*

AMANI: I thought it was immigration. Shit.

> YOMAL *enters. He draws a TV on a Perspex screen and sits on a stool to watch it.*

> HADIJA *enters. She draws a TV on a Perspex screen a sits on a stool to watch it; she circles her stool and looks occasionally at her screen.*

> TESAFAY *enters. He draws a TV on a Perspex screen a sits on a stool to watch it, using a remote control.*

> HAYDAR *enters and sits, his head hanging down; he checks his phone now and then.*

TESAFAY: [*repeating fragments of advertisements to himself*] Call, call carpet call, the best one in the trade! Want to see Jenny naked, call 1300… Authorised by the Australian Government Canberra…

> *Soundscape: 'Tom and Jerry' cartoons.*

SCENE TWENTY-SIX: IMMIGRATION BUST

Continuation of previous scene.

YOMAL *is laughing at 'Tom and Jerry'.*

HEIDI: [*bursting into the space*] Yomal, Yomal, immigration is here and they are coming up the path. Father Stevens gave them the key to get in. Quick, what are you gonna do?

> YOMAL *and* HEIDI *look for a place to hide.*

Quick, the kitchen. No, get in the bathroom; I'll pretend I'm having a shower.

> FEDERAL POLICE OFFICER *bursts in the space; he flashes his police ID. He approaches the audience the idea being to create the feeling that the federal police are raiding the actual performance.*

FEDERAL POLICE OFFICER: Is this Trades Hall *Journey of Asylum – Waiting*, the performance? I'm from the Federal Police and I'm looking for a Mr Prayintha. He's in this performance, have you seen him? Mr Prayintha; Yomal Prayintha. Is he here; do you know him; is he here; where is he; when did you last see him?

> *The* STAGE MANAGER *intervenes, informing the officer that 'we' are in the middle of a performance.*

Well, since no-one knows him, you won't mind if I look around.

> *The* STAGE MANAGER *starts to argue with the officer. The officer ignores him and heads for a door.*

HADIJA: There's a woman in the shower.

FEDERAL POLICE OFFICER: [*knocking*] It's the Federal police, can you open…

HEIDI: What, excuse me, I'm in the shower; who are you?

FEDERAL POLICE OFFICER: What's your name?

HEIDI: Natalie.

FEDERAL POLICE OFFICER: Okay, Natalie, I am from the Federal police and we are looking for a Yomal.

HEIDI: I don't know where he is.

FEDERAL POLICE OFFICER: Do you know him?

HEIDI: Yes, but I haven't seen him for days.

FEDERAL POLICE OFFICER: Okay. I'll leave a card out here and if you see him can you get him to call me? It's very important.

HEIDI: Yeah. Okay.

FEDERAL POLICE OFFICER: [*walking towards the audience, holding a card*] Okay, so I'll leave you all a card; the dob in line number is on the back.

He exits.

HEIDI: [*coming out*] He's gone now; we can get on with the show.

YOMAL *comes out, warily.*

All exit except MEMBER.

SCENE TWENTY-SEVEN: DETENTION

AHMAN *and* DOROTHY *enter.*

AHMAN *sits and begins drawing a picture on a Perspex screen; as he sketches,* DOROTHY *tells the following story.*

DOROTHY: The visitors' area. Maribyrnong Detention Centre. Friday afternoon, 2003. Emma, Lynne and I visit Ahman Bage, a Pakistani political activist. Been in detention for four years. A father figure; a mentor to many. Walks with the aid of crutches. Also a very talented sketcher. Tonight, at midnight, two boys are being sent back to Afghanistan. They are always taken at midnight. They've asked Ahman to sketch a gift for their families. Helen, a guard (who we are all afraid of), sees Ahman sketching, tells him to hand over his pad and pencil.

Ahman says, 'Why?' She says, 'You're not allowed have that here unless you've asked for permission'. So he asks, 'Can I have permission?' She says, 'No. You should have asked before'. He says, naming the two boys, 'They are going back tonight, and they asked'. She says, 'I don't care, give me your pad'. 'No I won't', says Ahman.

Helen reaches down rips the pad and pen out of Ahman's hand and proceeds to tear each page into small pieces littering them as she goes. Ahman remonstrates. Helen says, 'I'm not interested in anything you have to say'. Ahman stands and smashes his crutch through a glass window, littering us all with small fragments of glass. Helen presses the security button and four guards arrive. They drag Ahman, minus his crutches, off behind the guarded door. That was 2003.

DOROTHY *and* AHMAN *exit.*

ASLAM *enters, singing to himself.*

ASLAM: One hundred men locked up; frustration and fights; smoking cigarette after cigarette after cigarette; years of detention; counting days, nights, minutes, seconds… Sometimes we'd play volley ball. One TV, one hundred men.

NADIA *enters, singing to herself.*

MEMBER: Aslam, you're free to leave the detention centre. We can have you on the next plane to Pakistan.

ASLAM: But I'm Afghan.

MEMBER: Based upon my research into Afghanistan, you don't look like a typical Afghani.

ASLAM: Of course I'm from Afghanistan. I could name any street in Kabul. It's my city.

NADIA *sings.*

All exit except MEMBER.

SCENE TWENTY-EIGHT: CASE REJECTED

ANGEL *and* LIONEL *enter. Both have a plate of cake and can barely talk for too much cake in their mouths.* ANGEL *is in a happy mood and laughing as she overeats.*

ANGEL: Australia, the land of blessings, the land of free cake.

LIONEL: Free cars.

ANGEL: This is Australia. This is Australia. Aussie, Aussie, Aussie!

ANGEL: [*receives a call*] What… rejected? I was refused… I have to go to tribunal, tribunal…

ANGEL *runs to the Perspex screen where* ANDY *earlier drew maps.*

My god, I was rejected. Africa, Africa, I don't even want to see you on the map.

She rubs ANDY*'s drawings off the screen.*

ANGEL: Rejected.

LIONEL: I know.

ANGEL: We're going back to Africa.

LIONEL: No.

ANGEL: Oh, Jesus, I lose… [*Gesturing for* LIONEL *to sit down on the ground with her*] Hey man, I got a good idea; we need to go to the beach. You don't know how to swim… we just go past the yellow flags, that's it.

LIONEL: Do you know the size of a shark's teeth?

ANGEL: I got a better idea. Do you know the train—it's fast and it can't stop—this is another way. Just jump and we're finished.

LIONEL: Do you wanna see my brains out?

ANGEL: Okay, look, you see my house, it's got two levels, right? We can go upstairs and jump down—splat, finished.

LIONEL: The leg can go in the stomach, no no no no… I can't do this, man.

ANGEL: Look, I got the best idea, you know animal tablets?

LIONEL: Which ones?

ANGEL: The ones they give horses for races. You just swallow it and sleep indefinitely.

LIONEL *starts to be convinced.*

No pain.

LIONEL: I think that's a good idea.

ANGEL: That's why you're my friend, man, cause if they send us back to Africa we are finished. Australian immigration, you are that shark, you are that train, you are that fucking animal tablet.

ANGEL *and* LIONEL *exit.*

SCENE TWENTY-NINE: MOTHERS

MERRYN *enters with a file and climbs the ladder.* HADIJA *enters and faces the audience.*

HADIJA: Do you have children?

MERRYN: Yes.

HADIJA: How are old are they?

MERRYN: Twenty, fourteen, twelve.

HADIJA: My eldest is fifteen, second one is twelve, the younger one nine. What did you do on the weekend?

MERRYN: My girls go to circus training, go shopping and cook together.

HADIJA: Do they go school?

MERRYN: Yes.

HADIJA: If I see a woman walking with her child in the street or park; a family with their kids at McDonald's; children in the street with school bags… I'm just looking, or I see children on TV… give me pain, makes me very sad.

MERRYN: Where are your children?

HADIJA: My children are in Turkey.

MERRYN: And the father? Who takes care of them?

HADIJA. No father, no grandparent, no uncle, no auntie. They are alone. Sometimes I can't eat cause I'm thinking they're very young… can't cook… maybe they're sick. It stops my brain.

MERRYN: It says here that the Minister sent you a form for permanent residency two years ago.

HADIJA: Process, process, blah, blah, blah. Two years passed and no news, nothing. I've been waiting for permanent visa for three years.

MERRYN: Don't worry. I'm sure it will be over soon.

HADIJA: Lawyer, caseworker, manager, immigration, psychologist, nice people, lovely people! They say, don't worry, short time, everything is all right, but they don't understand. One day is like one year. My kids ask me, 'When we coming when, when, when?!' Sometimes I can't answer because the questions make me crazy. I go crazy, not for the visa but for my kids. Four times I stay in hospital, mental hospital, four times. Sometimes I am talking, I am laughing, but I'm not here, just my body is here. My daughter called me, 'Mum, you stopped the medication, please Mum, we love you, please start medication again'. And I start.

All exit except MEMBER.

SCENE THIRTY: THE TRIBUNAL

Screens are placed like a barrier behind the PROTAGONISTS, *who are seated in one long, straight line. It is a refugee review tribunal.*

TRIBUNAL MAN: The tribunal has now recommenced at 9.15 pm.

MEMBER: There are some serious discrepancies between the evidence you gave at your initial Department of Immigration and Citizenship interview and what you have said so far today. The inconsistencies are such that I might have to conclude that you are not a refugee. On the sixteenth of December, a field officer from the Department of Immigration went to the police station in your home country where you claim to have been detained. They spoke to a police officer and showed a photo of you. That police officer said he did not recognise your photograph or have any record of you.

TSEWANG: We were locked in a cell with maximum room for twenty people, but there were sixty of us. If the guards heard one person say 'Free Tibet' they would just pull that person out and beat them.

MEMBER: But you are not on their records.

TSEWANG: They will do anything to keep face. I have the medical reports.

MEMBER: How do we know that you didn't just hurt yourself?

TSEWANG: Why would I hurt my own face? I love my face.

MEMBER: In your first statement you said there was an attempt on your life on the fourth of April. Now you're saying it was the fifth. You're being inconsistent once again.

OMAR: You've asked me to explain twenty-four years of my life in two hours. The most painful moments of my life, when everything was at risk, the moments I need to forget. You're punishing me for trying to forget.

MEMBER: My role is simply to apply the law in a fair and consistent manner, not to make any personal judgements of you.

OMAR: I know what you're asking me, but I'm telling you, it's not possible to give exact times and dates when you're running for your life. You don't make notes.

MEMBER: Would it be fair to expect that you would remember the times when you genuinely feared for your life? You would remember something like that, wouldn't you?

UBAX: I remember. I can't forget.

MEMBER: That's right, 'I remember, I can't forget'. They were your words, yes?

UBAX: But I don't have dates.

MEMBER: Don't have dates. 'I can never forget', these were also your words.

UBAX: I remember. It was a Friday and everyone was praying and they all died.

MEMBER: Fifteen years to prove your identity. You've failed to satisfy any immigration official of who you claim to be.

YOMAL: I don't even know when I was born. I don't even know who my parents are. Is it so hard for you to understand?

MEMBER: The responsibility lies with you to prove identity, not with the tribunal. What was the name in your passport?

AMANI: I don't know.

MEMBER: If you travelled on this false passport, how can you not know the name you used? How can you now prove to me this is your real name? How do I know you're not actually Kenyan?

AMANI: I spent most of my life in a refugee camp in Kenya. I'm on the UNHCR computer system! I am Somalian!

MEMBER: You're claiming that they tortured you. You're claiming that they pulled out your toenails. That's a very serious claim to make. I want to see. Take off your socks.

ZAID *protests.*

Evidence, I need objective evidence. I want you to have a fair hearing but that requires you proving your claims. Please take off your socks.

ZAID *feels humiliated. Others sense his discomfort.*

They look fine to me. I don't think you've been tortured. I think you are making it up. You weren't high ranking, or an organiser for the MDC. Why would you be at risk?

LIONEL: I don't like their violence, what they stand for.

MEMBER: We have reliable country information that advises your country is now safe to return to.

ANGEL: From a website? You got information about Rwanda on a website? Have you ever travelled to my country? How can you make a decision on my case using a website? That's wrong.

TRIBUNAL MAN: The Internet is reliable.

MEMBER: You're a musician, you sing songs.

TESAFAY: Yes, I am.

MEMBER: And yet you're claiming to have been attacked for political reasons?

TESAFAY: Yes, I am.

MEMBER: That's what you're claiming.

TESAFAY: [*stands to show his scars*] What about this, I've been stabbed; I've been hit on the head.

MEMBER: I would never want to judge you, but what sort of a mother leaves her children behind?

HADIJA: If I had no problem, I would not leave my children for one day.

MEMBER: You do understand that you are under oath here? There are criminal penalties for lying in the tribunal.

> TRIBUNAL MAN *takes a document to* VIENNA.

VIENNA: Yes, I'm aware of that.

MEMBER: That's your signature, is it not?

VIENNA: Yes.

MEMBER: In your statement when you first applied for protection, there is no mention of any rape.

VIENNA: It's not something you want to tell everybody about.

MEMBER: Who told you to say you were raped? A friend? Your migration agent? Did you realise you couldn't win immigration status and so you decided to make a stronger case?

> VIENNA *is stricken.*

You claim persecution, for being homosexual. It's one that often appears in claims from your country. So can I ask you to name five songs by Madonna, please?

AHMAN: I beg your pardon?

MEMBER: If you were gay you'd know this. Well, do you go to any gay bars?

AHMAN: No.

MEMBER: Do you call any gay chat lines?

AHMAN: No.

MEMBER: Well, how can I believe you are gay?

ANGEL: My God, who gives you a qualification to do this job?

OMAR: [*interjecting*] If I name five songs by Madonna am I gay?

MEMBER: Why are you really here?

ALI: Why am I here?

MEMBER: You either came here for a better life or because you're a refugee.

UBAX: We are refugees, searching for a better life.

MEMBER: I don't need a lecture about refugees. I am well aware of what a refugee is. The question today is whether or not you are one. Before I wind up today's hearing and make a final recommendation, one final statement from each person.

ANGEL: Listen, can I pay for good decision, twenty thousand Rwandan money?

MEMBER: This is not Africa, mam. Next.

TSEWANG: This is a great country, sitting here are engineers, social workers, journalists, musicians. You could do so many good things, but to leave people in a state without the right to work or study is just stupid.

ISMAN: Why do I have to wait so long for a decision?

ALI: This is an advanced, modern way of killing people. Dangerous because you can't see, it's all hidden. How do you select who stays, who goes? The process is hidden.

MEMBER: Thank you. Next.

VIENNA: I came here for help. If you don't want to help me then why did you bomb my country? It is your responsibility to protect me; where do we go? If I don't get accepted I'll kill myself right here, right now. And the blood of my people will be on your heads.

> ZAID *rises in frustration and protest; he rips open his shirt, and a gesture that pleads 'what more do you want from us'; he speaks in Arabic simultaneously with* VIENNA.

MEMBER: Security.

TRIBUNAL MAN *and* SIMON: Security.

Two COLLABORATORS *remove* ZAID *from the room.*

AHMAN: People are not joking. Don't try to play with our lives, it could be dangerous.

MEMBER: Next.

HADIJA: In Australia everyone says, democracy, yes! But I think not, cause you can't speak. Instead, waiting, waiting, just waiting.

MEMBER: I am here to apply the law in a fair and objective manner in accordance with the *Migration Act* and the Refugee Convention. Next.

OMAR: You see how my hands sweat. Our lives look like a movie to you and your movies are our lives.

MEMBER: Thank you. I will not be making a decision today. You will be notified in writing. I will hope to finalise your matter in the next four to eight weeks and you will hear of my decision then. Thank you all very much. I wish you all the best in Australia and your life here. Good day to you all.

All exit except MEMBER. *Black out.*

SCENE THIRTY-ONE: PERMANENT RESIDENCY

TESAFAY *is sleeping inside the Perspex box. He wakes to listen to messages on this phone.*

HEIDI: [*standing in a spotlight*] Hi Tesafay, this is Heidi from the ASRC, um, Tesafay, I am finally calling with good news. The Minister for Immigration has granted you a humanitarian visa. Congratulations, Tesafay, we've been struggling for a long time but we've finally made it. Give me a call. Bye.

TESAFAY *replays the message.*

Hi Tesafay, this is Heidi from the ASRC, um, Tesafay, I am finally calling with good news. The Minister for Immigration has granted you a humanitarian visa. Congratulations, Tesafay, we've been struggling for a long time but we've finally made it. Give me a call. Bye.

TESAFAY *replays the message again.*

Hi Tesafay, this is Heidi from the ASRC, um, Tesafay, I am finally calling with good news. The Minister for Immigration has granted you a humanitarian visa. Congratulations, Tesafay, we've been struggling for a long time but we've finally made it. Give me a call. Bye.

TESAFAY: Oh, thank god.

He prays.

Black out.

SCENE THIRTY-TWO: THANK YOU CARD

IMMGRATION OFFICER *sits working.* LIONEL *knocks.*

IMMIGRATION OFFICER: Come in. What can I do for—
LIONEL: [*hands officer a card*] A card, thanks.

IMMIGRATION OFFICER *reads it. He is touched but puts on a professional exterior.*

IMMIGRATION OFFICER: Thank you. [*He stands to shake* LIONEL*'s hand.*] All the best.

THE END

Nothing But Nothing

TOWFIQ AL-QADY

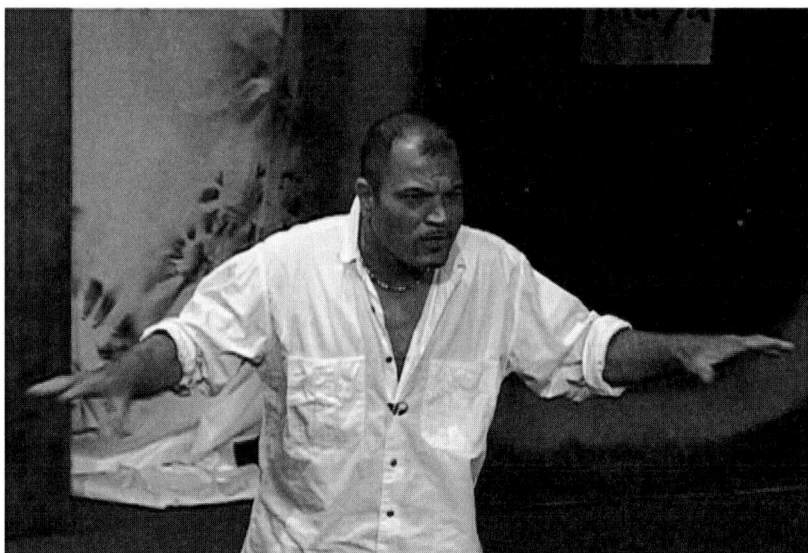

Towfiq Al-Qady as Actor in the 2005 Metro Arts Theatre production of Nothing But Nothing, *in association with Actors for Refugees, Queensland, in Metro Arts Theatre, Brisbane. (Photo: Faramarz K-Rahber.)*

Introduction

Towfiq Al-Qady's voice in his autobiographical work, *Nothing But Nothing*, is an emotional, sentimental one. His remembrances of childhood, of successive wars in his homeland of Iraq, the deaths of loved ones, a treacherous boat journey to seek asylum in Australia, detention and eventual 'freedom' are presented in language that glides across times, tenses and perspectives. These slippages allow Al-Qady to generalise his experiences, to graft them with the suffering of others, and even occasionally to speak *as* others. His self-presentation at one point even acquiesces, wryly, to an orientalist stereotype of the Middle Eastern voyager: 'Please write down my name is Sinbad'.

Like his performances in the 2005 production at Brisbane's Metro Arts Theatre, Al-Qady's text produces a free-flowing, stream-of-consciousness effect, but this belies painstaking composition. For Al-Qady, that meant using a language that was not native to him as a vehicle for communicating painful memories (he received some help with English translation from directorial assistant Leah Mercer). Bearing in mind Leigh Gilmore's observation in *The Limits of Autobiography: Trauma and Testimony* (2001) that 'Language is asserted as that which can realize trauma even as it is theorized as that which fails in the face of trauma' (p. 7), Al-Qady's translation of self is all the more remarkable.

Al-Qady's narrative doesn't fit the mould of legalistic testimony, nor did he adhere to common performance codes for verbatim theatre. How often are verbatim texts poetic, metaphorical, even self-mythologising? There is a widespread perception that 'emotional' and 'reliable' are incompatible adjectives. This is something Holocaust survivor Primo Levi recognised, stating in an afterword to an edition of *If This is a Man* and *The Truce*, 'I have deliberately assumed the calm, sober language of the witness, neither the lamenting tones of the victim nor the irate voice of someone who seeks revenge. I thought that my account would be all the more credible and useful the more it appeared objective and the less it sounded overly emotional' (p. 382).

How, then, do 'we' English-speaking, western readers who are in many cases all but allergic to melodrama and sentiment approach a text as unashamedly earnest as Al-Qady's? One that appeals directly to an audience's pity and sorrow? Indeed, precisely the type of representation of refugee identity that many writers and critics warn against, given that a preoccupation with suffering, loss and victimhood can all too easily, in Canadian theatre practitioner and scholar Julie Salverson's words, sustain 'the psychic residues of violent histories, codifying the very powerlessness they seek to address' (p. 35). With reference to protests and street performances by East Timorese refugee communities in Sydney during the long struggle for independence, sociologist Amanda Wise notes that Australian spectators tended to be 'most receptive to a certain kind of East Timorese diasporic identity that emphasized the suffering of exile as a particularly moral state of being' (p. 119). At the same time, Wise acknowledges the inescapable centrality of trauma within the East Timorese refugees' lifeworld, observing, 'the word "trauma" is familiar currency in the community' (p. 93). From a readerly perspective, Al-Qady's recourse to raw emotional exposure could serve to remind us that irony or circumspection may be *luxuries* when it comes to the portrayal of traumatic histories.

If Al-Qady's victimhood risks eliciting uncomplicated pity from a readership comprised mostly of Australian citizens in whose name the federal asylum mechanisms operate, it is worth remembering the power embodied by his face-to-face appeals to his audience at the Metro Arts Theatre—which were well attended by Australian-born and Iraqi contingents. In performance, Al-Qady's self-presentation as victim didn't constitute the surrendering of political voice, but rather, a direct request to his audience for attention and response. His use of interactive, questioning techniques pushed beyond conventional spectatorship; as I argued in a 2008 article on *Nothing But Nothing*, while audiences of his shows had, by 'attending the performance, implicitly consented to hear his testimony' and it is a stretch to claim 'that the contingency implied by his request is literal; what his gesture invokes, rather, is the context of alterity within which asylum seekers and refugees must speak' (p. 195). What Al-Qady's audiences heard was a unique play that is a 'true story' of the writer's life and at the same time a deeply romantic collage of memory, imagination, family, home and new beginnings.

Emma Cox

Nothing But Nothing was first performed by Metro Arts Theatre, in association with Actors for Refugees, Queensland, at the Metro Arts Theatre, Brisbane, on 10 April 2005, with the following cast and director:

ACTOR: Towfiq Al-Qady
MUSICIAN (OUD): Taj Mahmoud

Directorial and language assistant: Leah Mercer

PLAYWRIGHT'S NOTE

Nothing But Nothing: voices, memories, events, thoughts. I lived this; I heard it from friends when we escaped together from one land to another land, and from one airport to another, and from port to port, and in the detention centre. All these things live in my memory and I didn't have any difficulties with the writing. I wrote very quickly and very easily. I wrote this play in my everyday language so that I could be closer to the audience and tell a story that is true. I hope you will accept this play and hope you will enjoy it.

SETTING

A very large, wooden structure of the word 'NO' is positioned up stage, centre. White back lighting against the 'NO' structure produces shadows and shapes, which the actor uses to indicate different places such as his house, work place, etc. One actor plays different characters such as mother, friend, kids, etc. A musician plays instrumental music, either on or offstage. The actor is dressed in white and wears no shoes. He carries a handbag containing water, toothpaste, a wallet and paperwork.

ACTOR: Good evening and welcome everyone, I would like to thank you for coming tonight. I am happy to see some of the people I know and all the new faces. At the end of tonight I will be happy if we all become friends. Will you be happy with that?

He pauses for the audience response. The actor asks the audience different questions, attempting to draw as many 'yeses' as possible.

Tonight I am going to tell you a story about my friends and I will provide you with an image of my life. I will try to paint my incomplete painting, my story, in front of you, would you like that?

Audience responds.

I have spent all my life between yes and no.
It has been a very long journey.
Full of narrow points, between life and death.
The word 'yes' seemed never to be said. It seemed that all the doors for 'YES' were closed, but the doors for 'NO' remained open all the time.

ACTOR *stands in the light filtering through the letter 'O' of the wooden structure, then emerges from the stomach as if he is being born.*

As a child I opened my eyes and saw the beautiful sun smile at me.
I wanted to draw.
I drew the lines of my life, or so I thought; it was beautiful, happy, pure.
But at night I would miss my friends.
I would ask, where are my friends? Why did they leave? Are they ever going to come back?
The darkness seemed to always say, 'no'.
One day I went with my mum to a shop and I saw brushes and colours and that was the first time I wanted something badly.

ACTOR *starts walking among audience as if they are fellow shoppers at a shopping centre.*

I picked out a lot of things that I needed for my painting.

191

ACTOR *talks to his mother.*

Mum, I need these things for my painting.

She says, we can't afford to buy them. Because we don't have enough money.

Why don't we have enough money?

Because we are poor.

Why we are poor and some kids are rich? My father and teacher told me we are a rich country, and we have oil. My dad works and he has a job. Why are we still poor?

ACTOR *runs around the theatre, like a child is playing in the playground.*

I am a child, I like to play,
   with everything,
   I like to play soccer, and play the guitar.
   I would like to be an artist,
   I want to draw,
   I draw my dreams in my mind,
   I draw special places.
   But they disappeared.

ACTOR *looks suddenly confused, lost, and scared.*

The sky became filled with black smoke and weapons, tanks, soldiers, guns, shrapnel, blood. There is no sun, no flowers, no birds.

ACTOR *takes on two roles, mother and son.*

Mum, where is my dad? I miss him.
   She didn't reply.
   At school kids were asking each other,
   did your dad come back?
   Some said yes and others said no.
   After school, I went home and asked my mum again.
   She hugged me, I started to cry. I knew that something was over.

ACTOR *bows in front of 'N' as if it's a grave.*

Dad, Dad I miss you.

Every morning I wished to visit my dad in his new home and sometimes I wished I was there with him.

Dad I love you, I miss you.

When will you come back?

All of my friends ask me about you.

DAD!

Please come back, I dearly miss you.

Please come back.

You've taken too long.

Please Dad, come back.

But the emptiness of his room said 'no'.

And the places that are empty of his voice also said 'no'.

ACTOR *becomes downtrodden and depressed. He sits in the 'O' of the NO.*

I want to speak with my mum.

I want her to hold me tight as she sings to me a beautiful song.

ACTOR *sings a song in Arabic*

Oh, son, I love you but I am worried.

My son, stay with me forever.

My son, be my earrings, kiss me when I move.

My son, be brave, don't be weak.

When she finished her song, I asked her many questions.

I never got an answer.

I asked about my friends, my destiny, my dad, and about the noises.

ACTOR *looks at the 'O' as if it's a mirror.*

I'm a young man now, very strong, very happy.

I can do anything now.

No-one can tell me NO.

I feel strong. I can dream, I can sing, I have strength to do whatever I want.

I would like to be wealthy.

I'd like to be an engineer, to build houses and places for children.

I'd like to be a doctor to keep people from dying.

I'd like to be a poet, an artist.

I want to put an end to war.

ACTOR *plays two characters, that of the main character and that of an officer.*

This is not your job.

What is my job?

You should be a soldier.

What does a soldier do?

You will kill.

Kill who?

Other soldiers.

Why?

Because of the war.

Why not peace?

You will fight, and we will win, and we will be very rich and happy.

Impossible.

I know the war through the face of my mum. When my dad didn't come back. Even though you are very rich, you will be very poor because death follows you to your front door,

through the window,

in the car,

in the mosque,

in the church,

in school,

wherever you go.

I can't be a soldier.

I can't carry a machine gun.

I'd like to carry a paintbrush.

A guitar.

I can't kill the people. I'd like to draw the people's faces.

You can't be an artist and a soldier.

You should paint a mural for the great leader, Saddam Hussein.

And you will be very happy being a soldier and we will win the war.

I have two choices—either be a soldier, or go to prison.

ACTOR *goes to the 'NO' and drapes his body across it.*

I would rather be a prisoner than a killer or be killed.

I spent a very hard time in prison,
in Saddam Hussein's prison.
At that time, I preferred death than life in the prison.
They tortured me,
hurt me.
I spent my days in the darkness,
without sleep.
I have nothing, but sill remember the best thing I did:
painting.
I painted a dove with my fingertips on the prison wall.
The guard told the officer.
And the officer ordered me to wipe it off.
He said, if you don't wipe it off right now, I will make you wipe
it off with you tongue.
At that time I know that art was more powerful than prison.
More powerful than the government.
I was released from prison under some conditions.

ACTOR *emerges from 'N' as if from the bars of a prison.*

Shouldn't study art.
Must sign in at the police station.
Check in every day.
My name is black listed.
Not allowed to travel.
What could I do?
They told me to study economic management.
I started at the University of Baghdad.
I felt my heart was opening and warmth in my chest.
What is this?
Is this love?
Her name was Leila.
With Leila, I saw my dreams.
I liked her; I loved her, Leila.

ACTOR *speaks with Leila.*

Love me, we will build a house.
We can live in a house.
Love me, make my dreams come true.

Look, this is our love.

Leila, listen to me, please

Look at our circle, getting bigger, you will be my wife.

I will be your husband; we will have a baby boy and a baby girl, 10, 20, 200 and more!

Leila, let me finish my paining which will be the most beautiful painting.

There is you, myself, Mum, and Dad.

But there is a black dot in that centre that is turning and turning.

ACTOR *runs around stage, in a panic.*

Oh, Leila, Leila, run, the war…

Quick, Leila,

Leila, the war, the war,

quick, come with me, hug me,

stay with me and we will challenge the war,

our love, Leila, kiss me.

Leila, I will miss you.

No for love, no for a beautiful life.

War destroyed everything.

Destroyed my life, my love, Leila's house.

And she died with her brother.

What could I do?

Now my dreams are so small and I have nothing in life.

I am empty without my brushes, my job, my dreams, without anything.

'NO' followed me a long time.

I started to write poems, and I changed the mind of a soldier.

I said to him, throw your gun away,

and come have coffee with me,

and be a human being.

But the killing went on.

I continued with my life. I fell in love again and married and had a family.

1990, the Gulf War. Saddam Hussein appeared on TV and said, my people, another war is coming. I will need my people to be ready to fight. This is a big war. We will fight it against the whole world. And any Iraqi person who doesn't fight will be executed.

All Iraqi people were very busy with this war. I saw my daughter watching TV and all of a sudden, all the TV shows were about war. All the programs, songs, cartoons, and news were about the war. Saddam often appeared to talk about the war. I asked my daughter, 'why are you watching TV?' She didn't answer.

ACTOR *plays two characters, the main character and his small daughter.*

But at midnight she came to me and she said to me,
Dad, I have some questions.
Can the war be stopped?
No.
Are you going to die like your father?
No.
Am I going to die in the war?
No.
I don't want to die. I want to live.
I said: we are going to survive this war.
After that, I had two choices, either be executed or be a refugee.
I will be a refugee.
The war caused so many problems; families torn apart and separated.
I asked my daughter if she knew what it means to be refugee. She was silent.
It means to start a new life, new country, new language, new culture.
It is complicated.
No, no, you can't come with me; you can't because I will go to an unknown place.
And I don't know what will happen to me.
No, don't say that, we will meet again.
It is difficult to say goodbye to my kids at this time.
Now it is midnight.

ACTOR *takes his backpack from behind and sneaks behind the 'NO', hiding.*

I will escape from my home, my city,
my country, my people.

I should change my appearance, my face, my identity, my documents, my clothes, everything.

Oh, where will I go?

I think I will find small place in this big world.

ACTOR *falls to the floor.*

I am tired now.

I am hungry.

I am thirsty.

I haven't had slept for three days.

Oh, my dad.

I have lost my country, now I feel like an orphan.

Oh, my mum.

I am very weak now. I can't be strong, I lost everything.

Oh, my daughter.

I don't know where I am.

I don't know where you are now.

Please, can I sleep here?

I just want to sleep.

Please, can I sleep in this alley?

Can I sleep in this corner?

Can I sleep on this footpath?

Thank you, thank you.

ACTOR *lies on the ground and is dreaming; he speaks in his sleep.*

Oh, my daughter... ahh, Sweden, Canada, Australia, airport, police, passport, police, Saddam, spy, police, guards, soldiers, agents, secret agents, security guards.

ACTOR *runs frantically through audience speaking to random people.*

Please, can you help me?

Please, can I contact my family?

Please, can I sleep here?

Please, can I work here?

I have no money.

I don't speak English?

Please, can I sleep in this church?

Please, give me a blanket?

It is cold.

Please, please, please, my God. What happened to this world?

Nobody said welcome to me.

I am not a stranger, I am from this world.

Let me in, I am a legal.

God, tell me please, I am legal, legal, legal.

Trust me, I am legal, believe me, I am legal.

ACTOR *points at the 'O'.*

You, boat, you are my choice.

You will be my country, you will be my home.

Oh, boat, you are very small, very weak. You are made from old wood, very old.

I know the cost of freedom is very expensive. It cost my country.

My family…

Friends…

Job…

My life…

Okay… go boat, go where you will go… Anywhere you go is away from the war.

I didn't sleep for a long time.

Let me sleep… sleep… let me dream.

Thank you, boat.

Good morning, sea.

I like you and I am scared of you at the same time.

You are very big, very deep.

Please be quiet and soft with us, we are weak people.

I've had enough suffering on the earth,

I don't want to suffer on the sea.

You have a nice colour, blue is beautiful.

Do you know, I am an artist?

I know all the colours but I don't know the colour of freedom.

Please help me to see freedom.

Now, I would like to write freedom on this water.

I would like to make a huge sculpture of the refugees of the world from this

water, to say to the world, look, look what the war has made for
the people.

Oh... now two weeks have gone by.

We still haven't reached freedom.

When will we reach freedom?

What happened?

Why is the boat stopping?

What has happened?

The boat has broken down.

The engine has stopped.

Children, don't cry, be quiet.

Now three weeks in the ocean.

We lost the way...

The wind will be our guide...

Please wind, help us... to go.

I am tired, I am thirsty.

ACTOR *opens the water bottle, it has very little water drops. He*
swallows the last, desperately.

Please give me water...

What happened?

Nothing to drink.

Water is finished.

No water!

Please sky... water.

We need water, make it rain... rain.

We are in the middle of the sea.

The water surrounds us... and no water.

Oh.... salt... salt... brine... the water.

Look, the children are sleeping, hungry and thirsty.

Oh... shark... shark... let the children sleep.

Let them dream of freedom.

Now... I am nothing... I don't have any hope.

My heart will sink here.

I want to see the freedom before I die.

Please freedom, come to my country.

Sorry my daughter, I didn't get the freedom.

I will die here with my dream.

I will die, I am happy because I didn't kill anyone.

Leila, I will come see you.

Water... freedom... water... freedom... life... water... life... freedom... freedom.

ACTOR *looks up, excited, and points weakly.*

What is... this is... oh... look, look, a butterfly!

Life, my friend... look, we have reached freedom.

ACTOR *becomes more animated, strengthened by the prospect of land. Points and leans toward land.*

Look to the sun, trees.

Thank you god, thank you sea. Thank you sun.

Brothers and sisters, come dance on the water.

We can relax. I like to sing.

I would like a house, and a new car.

Finally, we are rich!

Boat, I have on more request.

Please go back because many more are waiting for you.

Sea, please be quiet and gentle.

And my friends, go down, get out, this is the freedom we have waited for.

ACTOR *sits as if behind bars.*

What happened?

Where's the freedom?

Some mistake.

I think we have missed the road.

I want to see freedom,

I have an appointment with freedom.

Where's freedom?

I have to see the freedom. Yes.

I feel tired... wait, wait.

But I wait for a long time.

Please, do you know how many times I say PLEASE during my life?

Freedom... freedom.

Please help us forget.
Please open.
So I should wait.
Let me dream.
So I should wait.
Yes, okay.

ACTOR *speaks as if in interview with immigration officers.*

All right… yes… yes… my name.
I forget, I can't remember.
Please write down my name is Sinbad.
My number? Five million.
Five million refugees, they escaped from my country.
My address? Okay, please write airports, checkpoints, ocean, boat.
My problem?
I hate the war.
Current job, yes, I am an artist.
Yes, I have experience.
My ID, my scars, my body.
My documents, my humanity.
Yes, I have a question.
When will you open this gate?
You don't appreciate freedom
Unless you have been denied it.
It has been a very long journey between two words.

ACTOR *holds out each hand to the audience as he speaks.*

YES or NO. That is the question.

THE END

Bibliography

Agamben, Giorgio. *Means Without End: Notes on Politics*. Translated by Vincenzo Binetti and Cesare Casarino. Minneapolis and London: University of Minnesota Press, 2000.

Ahmed, Sara. *Strange Encounters: Embodied Others in Post-Coloniality*. London and New York: Routledge, 2000.

Bachelard, Gaston. *The Poetics of Space*. Translated by Maria Jolas. Boston, Massachusetts: Beacon Press, 1994.

Cox, Emma. 'The Intersubjective Witness: Trauma Testimony in Towfiq Al-Qady's *Nothing But Nothing: One Refugee's Story*'. *RIDE: Research in Drama Education* 13.2 (2008): 193–98.

'Executive Summary'. *A Certain Maritime Incident*. Commonwealth of Australia, 23 October 2002: www.aph.gov.au/Parliamentary_ Business/Committees/Senate_Committees?url=maritime_ incident_ctte/report/index.htm

Gilmore, Leigh. *The Limits of Autobiography: Trauma and Testimony*. Ithaca and London: Cornell University Press, 2001.

Jeffers, Alison. *Refugees, Theatre and Crisis: Performing Global Identities*. Houndmills, Basingstoke: Palgrave Macmillan, 2012.

Levi, Primo. 'Afterword: The Author's Answers to His Readers' Questions'. Translated by Ruth Feldman. *If This is a Man* and *The Truce*. Translated by Stuart Woolf. London: Abacus, 1987. pp. 381–98.

Marr, David and Marian Wilkinson. *Dark Victory*. Crows Nest, New South Wales: Allen & Unwin, 2003.

McKay, Jim, Geoffrey Lawrence, Toby Miller and David Rowe. 'Gender Equity, Hegemonic Masculinity and the Governmentalisation of Australian Amateur Sport'. *Culture in Australia: Policies, Publics and Programs*. Edited by Tony Bennett and David Carter. Cambridge: Cambridge University Press, 2001. pp. 233–251.

Norrie, Justin. 'Rock The Boat, Baby'. Review of *CMI (A Certain Maritime Incident)* by version 1.0. *The Sydney Morning Herald* 26 March 2004. p. 15.

Phelan, Peggy. 'Marina Abramovic: Witnessing Shadows'. *Theatre Journal* 56.4 (2004): 569–77.

Salverson, Julie. 'Transgressive Storytelling or an Aesthetic of Injury: Performance, Pedagogy and Ethics'. *Theatre Research in Canada* 20.1 (1999): 35–51.

Savige, Jaya. *Surface to Air*. St Lucia, Brisbane: University of Queensland Press, 2011.

Wise, Amanda. *Exile and Return Among the East Timorese.* Philadelphia: University of Pennsylvania Press, 2006.

Enhanced eBook of
STAGING
ASYLUM

A comprehensive exploration of asylum-seeker issues within contemporary Australia, *Staging Asylum* the eBook, includes:

- Six complete scripts, with commentary, as in the printed edition.
- Contributions from:
  - Julian Burnside, who explores the core legal issues associated with seeking asylum—both national and international;
  - Kon Karapanagiotidis, who shares the amazing success story behind the Melbourne-based Asylum Seeker Resource Centre;
  - Judi Moylan, who offers a concise history of Australian governmental policy regarding asylum seekers and refugees—from federation to present day;
  - Morteza Poorvadi, who speaks about his personal experiences on seeking asylum;
  - Dr. Joseph Pugliese, who looks at how the suicide of escaped detainee, Habib Waheedy, should be used to reflect more broadly upon our civic duties and responsibilities towards asylum seekers and refugees;
  - Dr. Zachary Steel, who discusses his *pro bono* work in detention centres as a psychologist;
  - Dr. Caroline Wake, who examines the refugee determination process as a form of performance—whereby the assessed must present a case to the assessor, while both parties often mislead and misjudge each other.